I0438182

# My Brother Tom

A Courageous Black Warrior Who Struggled
for Survival on the Streets of Washington D.C.

*The Biography of a Remarkable Man*

**Thomas E. Ware**
**1929-2007**

authorHOUSE®

*AuthorHouse™*
*1663 Liberty Drive, Suite 200*
*Bloomington, IN 47403*
*www.authorhouse.com*
*Phone: 1-800-839-8640*

*© 2008 James J. Ware Jr.. All rights reserved.*

*No part of this book may be reproduced, stored in a retrieval system, or transmitted by any means without the written permission of the author.*

*First published by AuthorHouse 6/19/2008*

*ISBN: 978-1-4343-5355-9 (sc)*
*ISBN: 978-1-4343-5356-6 (hc)*

*Printed in the United States of America*
*Bloomington, Indiana*

*This book is printed on acid-free paper.*

# DEDICATION

This book is respectfully dedicated to Wilhelmena Ware, a loving wife for (56) years. (Tom called her his best friend). To Mother Cora Ware, and Dad James Ware, Sr., who brought us into this world. To our sister Bee who joined us in April 1921, and left us in March 2000. Bee was the moral advisor to the family. To our sister Doris, who was born in February 1923, and died in December 1984. Doris was the quiet, deep thinker in the family. To our sister Grace whose sunrise was December 1924, and sunset was January 1990. Grace was the social trend setter for the family. To our sister Helen, who boarded our ship in August 1926, and got off the ship in July 1982. Helen was the live wire protector for the family. To our cousin, Mildred, whom we called our 5th sister, she was born in June 1923, and died in June 2000. Mildred was the business oriented advisor for the family. To our young brother, Maurice, who was born in March 1934 and died in December 2007. He was a quiet church going armor bearer. And finally, to June Brown, Lois Armisted, Sara and Estelle Ellison; who grew up with us and supported us over the troubled waters.

# ACKNOWLEDGEMENTS

I would like to gratefully acknowledge the recipient of this book, Mr. Thomas E. Ware, along with Jasmine Geary, Lorraine Johnson, and Parrish Geary whose input and generosity made it possible for me to complete this publication without major difficulty.

Tom was my mentor counselor role model and sibling rival. When I published my first book," I'm Going Home on the Morning Train," Tom was the first person to purchase (25) copies. He then gave me critical advice on its' contents and encouraged me to get started on my next book very soon. Little did we know that the next book would be a biography of his remarkable life.

# TABLE OF CONTENTS

## III   On Being a Father

## IV   The Twilight Years

## Chapters

# I

# The Early Years

James Ware Jr. Age 2     Tom Ware Age 3

# Prelude to Poem
## MY BROTHER TOM

This poem was first delivered at Tom's funeral, and on the long flight home after the service, I started taking notes on all of the things I remembered about my big brother. I soon realized that I needed to write a book to capture all of his many accomplishments.

This poem portrays a mythical Indian Chief who can foretell the future. Tom and I used to laugh and joke about the old chiefs' words. The poem covers the early, middle, and twilight years of Tom's life. Hence, when you read the words, "Many Moons Ago," it is referring to Tom's early years.

# "MY BROTHER TOM"

Tell me Wise and Honorable Chief,
What can you say about my brother Tom?
Was he smart, was he thrifty, was he friendly, and was he strong?

The Old Chief looked up and said Hmmmm!
Big Tom, good friend of mine,
my talk about him may take plenty time.

Him always leader of the pack.
Him have keen insight.  Mentally, him sharp as a tack.

Him drive fancy red car with no top.
Him not worry about speeding tickets,
since him know most D.C. cops.

Him good speaker, him have gift of gab?
Him make good lawyer, for people in re-hab.

Him play base fiddle, him beat base drum,
Him sing and dance while making Xylophone humm.

Him dress well, him look good in his clothes,
Him match everything, from him head to him toes.

Him love railroads, have big job on trains,
Him always travel Amtrak, where him judge employee claims.

Him brave warrior in army, him courageous, him tough,
Him fight much harder when going gets rough.

Him travel to Africa, Brazil, and New York.
Him buy African paintings and fine art.
Him always buy good stuff, him never buy from Wal-Mart.
Him worked as correctional officer in D.C., reformatory,
Him controlled violent inmates in lockdown,
And counseled lightweight offenders in dormitory.

At age 15, him stopped you from bad habits.
You were drinking 39 cent wine and eating stolen cheese.
You stopped when he told you little Bro.,
"If you keep laying down with the dogs,
you will get up with fleas!"

Shame, you not listen to him and your wife,
When they tell you to lose weight, exercise and eat right.
Now you have lost both your kidneys,
and you must get transplant,
Or stay on dialysis for the rest of your life.


At early age, him good boy scout.
Meanwhile, him work on paper route.
Him try working as Western Union boy,
With heap better jobs, him buy more toys.

Him used to drink heap loads of super suds (beer).
Him kept baskets of oysters and crabs around
for his friends and peers.

Him later work for Secretary of Navy.
Where him eat good food, plenty steak and gravy.
Him glad to be away from eating in Military
Where him see fellow soldiers catch food poison and dysentery.

Finally, the wise chief said Brother James,
this is what I think of your Brother Tom,
"He is heap best thing that ever come along."

Honorable tribal leaders all say big Tom was clean
as Dapper Dan.
When him run ball on football field, him yell out,
"Catch Me If You Can."

In tribal council meetings, they all agree,
"Many moons ago," him tall, him dark, him have plenty money,
Him chase more women, than bee chase honey!

Remember, him tell you,
when Big Chief upstairs call him home to the sky's,
You sing no sad songs; you turn off water from your eyes.
You sing, happy song, "When the Saints Go Marching In,"
Him now free from sorrow, him now free from sin!

Lois, The Gastins, Best Man Tom and Litneal

Visiting Detroit, Mollie, Baby Jasmine, Maurice, Mother Cora
and Ronnie (Doris)

Mother Cora and the Ware Sisters Bee, Doris, Helen, and Grace.

A State Dept Official Willemena and Tom the U.S. Surgeon
General

Enjoying The Ware Family at 1201

Enjoying 3029 Clinton St. James, Maurice, and Tom

PVT. Thomas Ware U.S. Army

Making a purchase in Mildreds store in Detroit, happy Tom.

The Ware Boys: Tom, Maurice, James Brooks Ted and Mother Cora

A Man for All Seasons.

Tom and Maurice in California.

Tom and Wilemenna relaxing in Florida

Correctional Officer Tom Ware.

The Homestead 1201-G-Street NE

Tom and Wilemena crusing in the Bahamas.

We are somewhere in the crowd "Million Man March"
(Oct. 1995)

The Grand Old Patriarch Dad James Ware Sr.
Resting Between Jobs

# Chapter 1

### The Early Years

# WE ARE FAMILY

On a cold winter day in February 1929, in Washington D.C., our parents Cora and James Ware, Sr. smiled as the new arrival, baby Tom, kicked and yelled his way into the world (eight months later, October 1929, the country would suffer an economic blowout with the stock market crash). The family was glad to see the first boy since there were four girls that preceded him. Washington D.C. would never be the same since Tom hit the ground running. He dared to be different and he was not afraid of anybody or anything. The family was completed when I was born in October 1930, and Maurice joined us in March 1934. Our sisters made us understand that, "WE ARE FAMILY." We had a strong sense of family values and family pride. Our mother Cora Ware, was a strong spiritual family leader. She was loved by everyone.

From his early days, Tom had a strong keen of reasonable deduction. He would think about a problem before commenting on it.

When we were little guys, I remember Tom telling our parents what he wanted Santa Claus to bring him on Christmas day, afterwards he would tell me, "There is no Santa Claus, this is all a game, but I want my toys on Christmas day so I had to tell our parents what I wanted." Of course I said, "Yes, there is a Santa Claus, look at all the toys he brought us last year!" He said, "Alright, well you tell me how a group of reindeers can fly through the air with no engine power, or wings and how Santa brings all the kids on our block toys in his small sled, and how a big fat Santa Claus can slide down our small chimney?" I started to think maybe Tom is right. So we decided to sit on the stairs (in the dark) on Christmas Eve and wait for Santa to come down the chimney. We kept falling off to sleep and waking up all night long. Finally, early that morning we saw our parents taking the toys out of hiding and placing them under our tree. Santa Claus never showed up and we knew then that our parents were the real Santa Claus. We still rejoiced on Christmas morning.

Our big brother Tom was our mentor and role model. Every year when school closed for the summer, our parents sent us to Waverly Hall, Georgia, to live with our Aunt and work on the farm. Since our dad worked on the railroad, we could travel for free. Tom took care of us on the train and on the farm. He taught us how to take care of the one pair of shoes we received each Easter Monday (however, all kids in our age group went barefooted all summer long).

Tom woke up everyday with new ideas and plans for our future. As kids we would dream and make plans everyday. I remember saying to Tom, "Someday, I'm going to be a Millionaire." Tom said, "I will settle on being a Thousandnaire." We smiled when we realized that we had less than ten cents between the two of us.

## A HARD WORKER

Tom had a variety of jobs in his youth. He never had a problem getting a job. He was a busboy, Western Union delivery boy, janitor, printing press laborer and newspaper carrier. On his first job as a janitor in the local drugstore, Tom was tested for his honesty.

The store manager placed a ten dollar bill on top of the trash basket and gave Tom a list of duties which included emptying the trash. Tom saw the ten dollar bill and thought about what he should do. He decided to pick up the money and give it to the manager. He was elated when the manager said to him, "Son, you passed the test. We wanted to see if you are honest because we cannot have dishonest people working around us." As Tom shared it with me, I took the lesson to heart, but I was still an unreliable youngster.

## UNITED WE STAND

Our sisters drilled into us that, "WE ARE FAMILY." I must point out that the role of a big sister in a large family is very important. They assume the position of surrogate parents to the younger children. They washed our clothes, changed our diapers, fed us, walked us, clothed us and reported any ill health problems to our parents. Actually they gave us a double chance for survival. It also gave them on-the-job training for future motherhood. Each one of our sister's had a special talent and we knew which one to go to for our particular needs. If one were to ask, what was our parent's doing while the sisters were caring for us, Mother Cora was praying, cooking, sewing, shopping and watching over everybody. Dad Ware was working night and day, paying bills, buying us clothes and toys (whenever he could). It seems that everyone whose name was Ware had to dress up and go to Sunday school. Even today, each one of us has raised our family in the same manner. If we have weekend visitors, we take them to church with us, or they say good-bye on Saturday night.

As I reflect the years that Tom, Maurice and I shared as siblings, I am reminded of how close we were and yet what different personalities we portrayed. We shared the same lifestyle, ate the same food, exercised and played the same games, shared the same girlfriends and ran with the same street gang.

Tom followed the theory, "To Thine Own Self Be True." While I would always look at short cuts, I followed the theory, "Oh say can I see, what's in it for me." I was always suspected of criminal activity in our community. Tom was always respected and forecast as the one most likely to succeed. I am blessed that Tom's behavior pattern rubbed off on me and I changed my life for the better. I shutter to think that if I had not changed, I could be sitting in a prison cell today. "To God Be the Glory."

Maurice was the younger brother and we sheltered him. He was always quietly watching me and Tom interact. But he never joined in. Years later I said to Maurice, "Which one of your big brothers did you like to be around?" He answered, "Whichever one served the best fried chicken." As Maurice health went bad, Tom became his loyal caretaker and guardian. Eight months after Tom passed, Maurice joined him in heaven.

In another demonstration of his leadership skills at age seven, Tom joined the School Safety Patrol. As usual I followed him and joined the patrol. Tom was soon promoted to Captain of the patrol where he inspected us in our positions. We all wore silver badges, but Tom wore a gold badge.

I also followed him when he was hired on his first paper route. He encouraged me to take the route adjacent to his. Years later, I found out that he had transferred five blocks off of his route and added them to my route. I used to wonder how he would always finish his route before me, but I was too happy to have a job, so it didn't bother me!

As I reflect on the thousands of dysfunctional families that have been reared in poor communities in America, I feel lucky and blessed to have grown up in the Ware family, at 1201 "G" Street, Washington D.C. My brother, Tom, and my sisters came into this world with a mission to fulfill. They lived, fought and died as dedicated, faithful family members. I am still here today because they blocked out obstacles and paved the way for my future. I encourage all families to avoid issues of separation and unify for the good of the group. Get a firm spiritual foundation in your life and back each other up at all times. When the hazards of life get unbearable just say, Lord Jesus, thy will be done!"

*"I will Guide thee with mine eyes."*
Psalms 32:8

# Chapter 2

# A VALIANT WARRIOR

Growing up in Washington D.C. was like living in the Deep South during the 1930's. Washington was a segregated city, as well as the capitol of the USA. The population of the city was predominately Black. To us, the words "D.C.", meant "Dark Cloud." There were eleven high schools in D.C., and only three of them were designated for blacks. Unfortunately all three black high schools were located in Northwest D.C. Those of us, who lived in Northeast, Southwest, Southeast, D.C., had to walk to school. School buses were not available to us, and we could not afford the street car fare. Tom attended Armstrong High School on "O" Street, and I attended Dunbar High School, across the street on "N" Street. We would follow Tom to and from school everyday. If he played hooky from school, we did too. Fortunately for us, Tom was a positive role model, and he encouraged us to never play hooky. If Tom witnessed anything unusual along the way, he taught us to get tag numbers off the cars and make notes of any unusual activity.

During the hot summer days in D.C., black kids had to suffer it to be so! The swimming pools and movie theaters were totally segregated. The city provided some relief by mandating the local fire departments to turn on the street water hydrants to sprinkle us, and cool us down. They would only stay on your street for one hour, since they had a lot of streets to cover. On the hot sweaty days, Tom would lead us to the nearby Rosedale swimming pool, where we stood outside the fence and watched the white kids enjoying the cool water. One day Tom said, I want all of you to meet me at my house tonight. All twelve of us met him and followed him to the Rosedale pool. To our surprise, Tom climbed over the fence, jumped in the pool and started swimming. He then got out and encouraged us to jump in, which we did. He then acted as a life guard while he taught us how to swim. For the rest of the summer, we spent our hot summer nights enjoying midnight swimming. Years later I asked him, how, when and where did he learn how to swim? He said, "If they can do it, I can too," so I just did it and it came natural to me.

## FOLLOW ME

Tom was also instrumental in teaching us how to earn money by recycling discarded coke bottles, newspapers, scrap metal and rags. We called it hustling. We lived at 12th and "G" Street, and there was a junk yard located at 15th and "G" Street. Tom built a push cart which we used to make a daily junk run. We would divide up the proceeds from the sale of the junk (usually $3 or $4 dollars). Tom always got the largest share. He let us know that we were using his push cart and his ideas, and we had to pay for the privilege! We all agreed, since it gave us money to buy candy. We needed money, especially since our parents could not afford to give us a monetary allowance. We were pleased that they gave us plenty of food, warm clothing and a comfortable shelter. Such was the plight of young black youth growing up in D.C., in the 1930's.

The twelve kids that we grew up with could have been called the "Dirty Dozen" or the "Band of Twelve." They were local neighborhood kids. We were all in the same age group. We met everyday on the corner of 12th and "G" Street, where we shared experiences, told lies, and forecast our future. The group consisted of Tom Ware, Junior Ware, Maurice Ware, Bumpy Allen, Wade Allen, Wiley Marshall, Otis Johnson, David English, Robert Collins, Paul Waters, Chris Holmes, and Sonny Grant. We looked to Tom as our General. It is amazing how God blessed him to say and do the right things, at the right time. He demonstrated positive leadership. For example, I can still hear him say, "Follow me," as he led us to the Ringling Brother's Circus that was passing through our town. We learned how to get free passes to the shows by helping the roustabouts lift the tents and by helping the trainers feed and water the animals. While our experiences at the Rosedale swimming pool were memorable, we were blessed to witness the transition of the neighborhood. The system of "White Flight" began to take place, and the exodus of white citizens moving out to the suburbs caused the pools to open to blacks.

## A PASTORS LAMENT

On another occasion, we were all proud of our pastor, Bishop Smallwood Williams, who decided to sit in the classroom with his son, Smallwood, Jr., at the local, Wheatly Elementary, white school, located one block from their home. Bishop had moved into the white neighborhood with the help of friendly white realtors who "fronted" for him in purchasing his home (this system was used prior to the massive civil rights movements of the 60's). The year was 1952, Bishops' son, Wallace, was scheduled to be transferred from Charles Young Elementary School, about four miles from their home to Cromwell School which was not up to standard. Bishop challenged the system by staging the sit-in. His attorney told him he would not be arrested for trespassing because D.C. did not have a law applicable to trespassing on government property at the time (There is now a law covering government buildings). The incident made the headlines and messages of support were sent to him from everywhere, strangely enough, some blacks called him crazy, they openly stated, "Who does he think he is, trying to put his black child in a white school?" This made him more determined. The school board played games with him by moving white students into different classrooms, so he ended up sitting in the school hallway. The laws stated that the Bishop could be arrested if he disturbed the peace, so the superintendent tried to set him up by blocking the door when he came to the school the next day. They had two uniformed police standing by and if Bishop had touched him in attempt to enter, he would have been arrested. The Bishop quickly assessed the situation and turned away. He then realized that he would not prevail unless the segregation laws were changed. At the time there were more than 300,000 blacks living in D.C. and the black schools were over crowded, while there were large vacancies in the white schools. When a group of black parents sent a letter to the school board asking that the white schools be opened to blacks in the area, they were given the stock answer from the board "Sorry the law won't let us do what you ask." So Bishop turned to the courts for relief. By this time he was concerned about the emotional stability of his son, who played with the white kids in his neighborhood, but could not go to school with them. He paid a $1,000.00 dollars retainer to attorney James Nabrit to continue the fight. For the next few years the public was aroused, civil rights reports were submitted to the President and the Bishop continued fighting from the pulpit. Congress was deluged with letters and demonstrations, unions, and labor forces joined the fight to stop Jim Crow segregation in the Nations Capitol. The press from countries abroad got in the act. And finally on May 17, 1954, the Supreme Court banned segregation in public schools.

## HAPPY HALLOWEEN

In most communities, the children celebrate Halloween by going from door to door for candy saying, "Trick or Treat." In our community, most of the residents were far too poor to give out candy. So we created our own system and called it Trick and Treat." We kept up with those people who were not nice to us during the past year. We called their home a "Bad House." The good people lived in what we called a "Good House." David English kept records on the Good/Bad houses, and our leader, Tom Ware, made the final decision on which house was Good/Bad. Bobby Collins and I selected the dubious trick we would play! Bumpy Allen, Maurice Ware, and Otis Armstrong, gathered the materials we used in the trickery. Wiley Marshall, Christ Holmes, Paul Waters, and Wade Allen, were the strike soldiers that carried out the trickery. The tricks on the bad houses, included, placing a bottle of water over the top of the front door and tying it to the door knob, ringing the doorbell and yelling trick and treat when someone opened it. Placing soap all over cars, placing tape all over the front porch and making excessive noise. A house was good if the owner, baked us cookies, paid us ten cents to shovel snow or coal, paid us five cents to help them with groceries, although it would seem like we were little hoodlums. Every one of us would dress up on Sunday, and go to Sunday school. There were two local rival street gangs in our community, namely, "The 13th Street gang," led by Walter Fletcher, and, "The Wiley Court Street gang," led by Booky Williams. The gangs were competitive in baseball, track, football and snowball fights. However, we never carried guns or knives. In fact, our leader Tom, gave us a list of no-no's:

1. No stealing
2. No purse snatching
3. No disrespect to: Women/Elders/our Grandparents
4. No fighting or abusing younger Children/Elders/Family
5. No cruelty to animals
6. No carrying gun/knives/explosives
7. No starting fires ( arson)
8. No drugs
9. No playing hooky from school
10. No damaging people's property

We were a far cry from today's street gangs that require you to commit a crime before you can join them, or who attack each other if they wear the wrong colors. We did not wear baggy pants, turned around ball caps, extra large unfitting clothes or tons of jewelry. We could not afford to buy jewelry.

The winter months in D.C. were cold and wet, but we were use to it, and we enjoyed the snow. While the rest of our gang played and had snowball fights, Tom spent his time going from door to door, offering to shovel the snow off the sidewalk for twenty-five cents. He was always a sharp businessman.

I am pleased to say that, Tom always asked his employer to hire me along with him and so it was. At one point he suggested that we open a joint bank account where we could cash our checks and save some of our earnings. He convinced me to let him handle the banking transactions. I was a little perplexed when I discovered years later that he had made a number of withdrawals without my knowledge. Of course I never complained about it, because without his help, I would not have had a job, or a bank account. We also worked at the Bolling Air Force Base Officers Club as busboys. Tom was soon promoted to waiter and then assistant Chef Cook. I was given added duties as dishwasher with a small pay raise.

It is significant to note that during the past years, there have been more then 40,000 killings by gangs and gang members in large (American) cities. Most of the killings were in the Black and Hispanic communities. Thanks to our leader, Tom Ware, the "G' Street gang of twelve had a different set of goals and objectives. Tom was blessed with intuitive thinking and high moral values, and he led us down the right road.

As I reflect on our swimming experiences, I remember in August of each year, our Sunday school would sponsor a bus trip to Sparrows Beach (down on the Eastern shore of Maryland). All of the kids looked forward to a day of fun at the beach. One year our bus had an accident as we were returning home. While the rest of us were crying and screaming, Tom climbed out the window and helped us to exit the bus. He always seemed to know just what to do when something happened. The bus company gave him a monetary award for his bravery. Fortunately none of us was hurt in the accident. He was a gifted individual. He was a valiant warrior.

> ***I have fought a good fight, I have finished my course,***
> ***I have kept the faith.***
> 2 Tim: 4; 7

# Chapter 3

# WHY SHOULD WE RUN

Another one of the early signs of Tom's leadership skills was manifested during our corner experiences. As previously stated, our group sat on the same corner everyday. In later years we realized that we should have spent those hours studying and doing homework, but since there were no computers and the libraries were segregated, we lived as though life was all fun and games. Even in our classrooms at school, we were given soiled, used, textbooks, while the white schools were issued new text books. Our books were often defaced with the "N" word and with torn and mutilated pages enclosed. So we had our discussions and encounters on the corner. Tom always led our discussions, and he set the tone for us.

## STANDING UP

The highlight of our corner experience was the appearance of the local police who walked through our neighborhood at the same time everyday. Once in the morning and once in the afternoon. There were very few black policemen on the force at that time. The police officers were giant Irish men, who wore blue uniforms and carried a gun, big stick and handcuffs. They intimidated us with their huge gold plated badge and their slow walk. We could see them coming down the street about one block away from us. They were always walking. We hardly ever saw a police car except to pick someone up and take them to jail. As they got closer to our group, someone would yell "Police" and we would scatter and hide until they would pass us by, then someone would yell "All clear" and we would return to our corner spot. The whole action was an automatic reaction. One day Tom said we have not done anything wrong, "Why should we run, every time we see a policeman?" I'm not going to run anymore!! Nervously, I said, "If you don't run, I wont' run." Very shortly someone yelled "Police" and the group ran everywhere. Tom and I sat there with our knees shaking. We were scared as the police officer walked up to us, he said, "I'm glad you kids didn't run I want to talk to you. I always saw you run when I came near you. I saw where you were hiding and I watched you come back when I had passed by. Kids, I want you to be my eyes and ears for this neighborhood. Let me know if you see something illegal or wrong going on. You can be my junior cops!" He then gave us some candy and said goodbye. Needless to say, Tom became the neighborhood hero for not running from the police. I was still his able assistant.

## LET'S RUNAWAY

On another occasion, Tom decided he wanted to run away from home. He had read about other places and wanted to explore the happy green valleys away from 1201 "G" Street. He said, "Let's run away from home," and as usual I said, "Ok." So we packed two peanut butter sandwiches each and one apple and some saltine crackers in a paper bag and started on our way. Our sister's said goodbye to us after they warned us not to leave, but we were determined. By the time we got three blocks away, we had eaten half of the lunch and we were thirsty. We both decided this is not going to work and we turned around and headed back home. To our surprise, our sister's knew we would be coming back, and they never shared it with our parents. We never tried to run away again, especially when we learned that runaway kids were picked up and taken to the D.C. children's home. This (juvenile jail) was rampart with child abuse and unstable living conditions. The kids were poorly fed and accused of crimes they did not commit. I have first hand knowledge of the home since I spent two days there for being accused of breaking a neighbor's window. I was arrested because I looked like the boy that did it. I was very happy when my dad bailed me out, and I stayed close to the warm comfortable, 1201 "G" Street, for a long time afterwards.

In those days, we walked everywhere, including our elementary school, three blocks away, our Sunday school eighteen blocks away. The Saturday Cowboy movies twenty-two blocks away. None of us ever had an obese over weight problem. Our leader Tom would always encourage us to stay healthy.

## TRAIN UP THE CHILD

Our parents wanted us to have the best training that they could afford to give us. Some kids (not in our group) played little league baseball. We joined the Junior Elks and every third Sunday; we went to the Elks Lodge downtown, with our white shirts and purple sashes, where we were taught how to treat young ladies and other social graces.

One of the few times that I took over Tom's role as our leader involved a young kid who had just got a new bike and he was throwing his old bike away. I asked him to give it to me and he agreed. So I took the bike home and Tom helped me to clean it up, and we put on new tires and painted it. When we rode it out on the street, the kid was amazed at how it looked, and he demanded that I give it back to him. I spoke up and said, "Ok, you can have it back, provided you pay us for our labor and materials". He just walked away while Tom said, "Good job, brother."

The only time that I did not follow Tom was when he joined the Boy Scouts. I was not interested in joining. He was soon promoted to an Eagle Scout, and it enhanced his growth. In retrospect perhaps I should have joined the Scouts along with him.

Tom had an aggressive spirit. He was always ready for a fight. We fought at least three times a day. He would hit me or kick me, morning, noon and night, and I would hit him back. There was hardly ever a reason for the fighting. To my surprise, he shared with me his motive years later. He said he was teaching me to defend myself, by hitting me.

His system worked for me. As soon as I turned seventeen, I joined the Air Force and I had my first fight, the first week in basic training. The squadron bully was testing each cadet by hitting them. The weak cadets who did not fight back paid the price of humiliation the rest of our training months. As for me, I fought like a tiger, I fell down and got up fighting, he fell down and I fell on top of him kicking and yelling at him. The other cadets had to pull me off of him, and I heard one of them say, "Ware is crazy." For the rest of the training months they called me "Crazy Man Ware." I served in the Air Force for the next twenty-two years and I never had to fight a fellow airman again.

I must point out that our younger brother Maurice used to watch us fight everyday but he never got involved. I remember one occasion, where he hit both of us with a wooden board, and we attempted to hit him when our sisters stepped in saying, "Don't hit your baby brother!"

I shall never forget how our sisters especially, Helen and Grace, protected us. One day Walter Fletcher, (13th Street gang leader) hit Tom and was coming after me. He stopped when Helen and Grace came running out of the house yelling at him. Helen picked him up and Grace lifted up the street sewer top. Helen was going to throw him into the sewer. I can still hear her saying, "My brother, right or wrong, don't mess with him." The street gangs all understood that "We are family" and they respected our sisters.

## HOW CAN I FORGET

One of the biggest fights that I had with Tom, was over a sweet, charming little girl named "J.P." She was visiting our home one day and Tom and I were both amazed at how beautiful and graceful she was. She had on a red dress with a white bonnet and white shoes and she sat quietly and smiled while Tom and I struggled to sit next to her. I forgot to mention that Tom was about seven years old and I was about six years old at the time. As she was leaving our home, I said, "That's my girlfriend," Tom said, "No she's not, she's my girlfriend." I said, "She smiled at me," and Tom said, "She smiled at me too!" Tom said let's fight, and whoever wins the fight wins the girl. I said ok let's fight. Once again Tom had out-smarted me, because I had never been able to beat him in a fight. But I really wanted "J.P." to be my girlfriend. Just as we prepared to get at each other, our sister, Grace said, "Are you brother's crazy, J.P. is your relative and you don't fight over family." I said, but she smiled at me, and Grace said she smiles at everybody, that is part of her personality. Tom said, I don't care if she is family, "Let's fight." I said, ok, "Let's go." Needless to say he beat me, and I could not call her my girlfriend.

While gathered at a social setting many years later, J.P. and I were looking back over the years, and I said did you know that Tom and I had our biggest fight over you. She said yes I heard about it. And I said please tell me after all these years; please clear my mind, "Which one of the Ware boy's did you care for the most?" Well I lit up like a candle when she answered, "Junior, I always did like you," then the lights-out when she said, "But I loved Tom."

As we grew older our fighting was curtailed and one day Tom said little brother let's sign a truce, let's not fight anymore. I was glad to shake his hand and to stop fighting since I could not beat him anyway. Our mother Cora Ware,was happy for us. She called us in and prayed for us. We never fought again. I thank God for my brother, Tom.

*The Lord is my Shephard, I shall not want.*
Psalms 23:1

# Chapter 4

# SURVIVING WORLD WAR II

During the early 1940's, the war was taking its toll on all of us. Rationing food and gas, recycling scrap metal, papers, rags and glass bottles, conserving fuel and electricity, and saving nylon stockings and rubber tires was a top priority for all American citizens. We experienced blackouts at night, and Air Raid Wardens patrolled our streets. Tom was one of the first of our group to be appointed Junior Air Raid Warden. We were warned about possible food shortages as the war progressed. So Tom helped our father build a wood shed in our back yard, where we stored canned goods.

The war gave our family an opportunity to work on jobs that had been previously closed to us. Ten members of the Ware family had jobs working at the Washington D.C. train station, namely, Dad Ware, Estelle, Kenny, Red, Helen, Tom, Bernard, Mildred, Grace and Uncle Bot. Doris was the only member at that time who joined the Army WAC's (Women's Army Corps). She was sent to England and France where she served for three years. She is enshrined in the World War II Memorial for Women in the Military, at Arlington Cemetery. I remember how happy we were when she was discharged and came home. Tom painted a huge sign on our front door saying, "Welcome Home Doris."

Good Government jobs were plentiful and our relatives took advantage of the opportunities for employment. At one point during this time, there were five members of our family working at the Navy Department, namely, my sister Doris, my brother Tom, my wife (to be) Mollie, my brother-in law (to be) Wendell and my brother-in law (to be) James. Some of them car pooled it to work.

## DO THE RIGHT THING

It is no secret that the Ware family was spiritual and patriotic. We sold war bonds and stamps for our school. Our school received a certificate of outstanding sales and we purchased a 1944 Jeep for Military use. To this end, three Army Soldiers delivered the Jeep to our school and drove it up the front steps. Our Principal and a group of students dedicated it by painting a decal on it saying "Complements of Brown Jr. High School, Washington D.C."

To help with the war effort, the city started a Youth Victory Farm Program, where they recruited inner-city youth to work on the crops. Since most able-bodied men had gone off to fight in the war, the women and children had to carry the load. We had to sign up for two months during the summer. We lived in a school gym near the farms and we were not paid for the service. I volunteered to go, but Tom said he wanted to be paid for his labor, so he spent that summer working as a junior lifeguard (paid position). We actually worked along side German Prisoners of War who had been captured, and sent to the states until the war ended. I enjoyed the experience, however, I was unhappy to see the German Prisoners eating better food and living in better quarters than our youth group. When we complained about it, we were told that our group was sponsored by the city of D.C. while the German Prisoners were under the U.S. Government. We could not talk to the prisoners, but it didn't matter because they could not speak English and we could not speak German. We worked from 7:00 am to 3:00 pm each week day, picking, tomatoes, beans and spinach. The military police brought the prisoners to the farm from 8:00 am to 2:00 pm each day and we all picked the same crops.

## SUFFER IT TO BE SO

D.C. citizens did not always enjoy the wealth of good living as some might expect. Those who did not have good government jobs had to survive off minimum wages. The rent, insurance and bill collectors would haunt them every week-end to pay the small but hard to get money. Since the bills were always paid on Saturday morning. They had house parties every Friday night, to raise the money; every room in their home was used for fund raising. The activities included dancing, socializing, eating, and gambling. The hostess would walk around with a large mayonnaise jar marked "Feed the Kitty." Each participant had to contribute for participating in whatever they wanted to do. There was also a cover charge for you to pay to enter the home. For those citizens who were not fortunate in raising their rent money, they would often find their furniture placed on the sidewalk. They were evicted and the doors were pad locked. It was disheartening to see little children and adults sitting on top of all their earthly belongings all night long, guarding it from looters. Landlords showed no mercy. They would knock on your door for the rent money, if you did not pay them, they would signal for the "Kick them out crew" (A group of strong brothers) who would begin moving you out. There was no police eviction notice given in those days. For this cause, families had to double up and live together for survival. Another problem was the lack of affordable housing for blacks. (Presently, California is experiencing a large number of immigrants who are surviving by living combined in family houses). It was encouraging to later see the city change its ordinances and create more friendly laws regarding eviction notices in D.C.

## THE ULTIMATE SACRIFICE

Thousands of men and women were wounded or killed during World War II. As such, the Western Union Telegram Company was kept busy sending condolence telegrams to the bereaved families. A death notice telegram was flagged with three red stars. Subsequently, the death notices would be personally delivered by a Chaplain and commissioned officer who comforted the family. Both Tom and I were delivery boys. We were provided with a uniform and a brown bicycle. We were forbidden to say anything about the telegram to the family since we were untrained in how to console heartbroken people. I shall always remember hearing the loud cries of pain and anguish as I delivered a three star telegram and left the home. I always said to myself, bless them Lord.

## BUILDING AMERICA

Another one of Tom's jobs was working on the Pennsylvania turnpike, as an unskilled laborer. At one time more than 15,000 workers were building America's first super highway. The turnpike had its roots from William H. Vanderbuilt, who proposed to build a railroad under his control from Harrisburg to Pittsburg, Pennsylvania. After spending $10 million and with the loss of twenty-six workers killed, the work was stopped. It was known as "Vanderbilt's folly." In 1937, the Pennsylvania turnpike commission was enacted. The plan called for cutting seven tunnels through the mountains. Contractors had to work day and night, three shifts a day to keep on schedule. Most of the workers were Pennsylvania coal miners, who were on a strike from the Coal Miners Union. Four men lost their lives in a cave-in on one of the tunnels. The estimated cost for building the turnpike was 70 million. Some of the workers lived in tents. During the summer young boys were hired to carry water to the tunnel workers. Tom was the first one in our group to volunteer. When the summer ended, he came back home with what seemed to us to be a lot of money. He had earned enough money to buy himself a new wardrobe. He gave us his old clothes and we were happy to get them. Actually this was the beginning of his role as Mr. "G.Q" as he started wearing sharp clothes.

Tom was always willing to accept a challenge. He would take a job that was completely out of his range and he would soon master it. Again, I was always blessed to follow him. I remember when we worked at a publishing company, and we were assigned to a stitching the machine for magazines. We had to catch the magazines off the machine and stack them twenty-five to a stack. We had to move fast or the machine would overflow. Tom mastered the art within two weeks. I was transferred to the truck loading department after one week. I often remember Tom saying to me, "You must be more aggressive." "You have to call the shots." "You have to bite the bullet." "If you don't move up to the front, you will always be found in the back." God gave Tom an inner strength!

*Wherefore take upon you, the whole armour of God, that ye may be able to withstand in the evil day, and having done all to stand, stand therefore.*
Ephesians 6:13

# Chapter 5

# 1201 "G" Street. Northeast
# THE FAMILY HOMESTEAD

We grew up in the family home at 1201 "G" Street, Northeast, Washington D.C. Even today, I think about the happy times I spent in that hallowed home. During the 1930's, 40's and 50's, we lived under difficult strains. First, there was the depression, followed by World War II, the Cold War, and then the Korean War. Ironically our dad worked as "day laborer" cleaning the streets during the depression. Our sister Doris served in the army during World War II, and both Tom and I served in the military during the Korean War. The war years brought our family closer together. 1201 was considered a landmark (stop over point) for black families migrating from the South. They would stop in Washington, D.C. enroute to Chicago, New York and Detroit. They stayed with us at 1201, since hotels were not available. At one point, I counted five families with twenty-three people living in our four bedroom house. My mother told me that since I was the baby (at that time); she fixed my bed in the bathroom tub at night. Others slept on pallets on the floor. We converted the living and dining rooms into bedrooms. Some family members worked at night. Everyone contributed to the food, rent and utility bills, and everyone ate the same food at each meal. We learned to respect each other, and we made it work.

The following is a list of the Pioneer family members who lived in 1201, during the years (1930 - 1948):

**1st Family**
1. Grandfather H.Y. Ellison, Deceased
2. Grandmother Buford Ellison, Deceased

**2nd Family**
3. Father - James Ware, Sr., Deceased
4. Mother - Cora Ware Deceased
5. Daughter - Bernice Ware, Deceased
6. Daughter - Doris Ware, Deceased
7. Daughter - Grace Ware, Deceased
8. Son - Thomas Ware, Deceased
9. Son - James Ware, Jr.
10. Son - Maurice Ware, Deceased
11. Uncle - Bot Ware, Deceased
12. Niece - Yvonne Ware

**3rd Family**
13. Uncle - Richard Ellison, Deceased
14. Aunt Ella Ellison, Deceased
15. Cousin - Mildred Ellison, Deceased
16. Cousin - Estelle Ellison

**4th Family**
17. Brother-in-law - Bernard Plater, Deceased
18. Sister - Helen Plater, Deceased
19. Nephew - Bernard (Lamar) Plater, Deceased
20. Nephew - Morris (Pete) Plater

**5th Family**

    21. Cousin - Walther Neal, Deceased

    22. Cousin - Thelma Neal, Deceased

    23. Cousin - Elizabeth Neal, Deceased

Although there were a lot of us crowded together, we got along well. My dad called 1201, "The Ware Hotel." I left to join the Air Force in 1948. However, there were eighteen additional members of family that established temporary residence at 1201 from the years

(1949-1991). By this time, many of the original pioneer 23 members had relocated. 1201 was home to the following persons:

    1. Aunt June Ware, Deceased

    2. Brother-in-law James Kennedy, Deceased

    3. Cousin Robert Blount, Deceased

    4. Cousin Mae Belle Blount, Deceased

    5. Niece Doris (Ronnie) Plater

    6. Niece Janice Plater

    7. Niece Mary Plater

    8. Cousin Lois Ellison

    9. Cousin Betty Jean Ellison

    10. Nephew Harold (Red) Ware

    11. Brother-in-law Jim Johnson

    12. Nephew Anthony Johnson

    13. Nephew David Johnson, Deceased

    14. Nephew Dennis Johnson

    15. Cousin Iverson Neal, Deceased

    16. Cousin Jessie Neal

    17. Cousin Angela Neal, Deceased

    18. Cousin Mack Neal, Deceased

In spite of our crowded conditions, we were elated to have Duke Ellington spend one night in our home. The Duke was performing at the Howard Theater, and there was no available vacancy at the Dunbar Hotel where most black entertainers stayed while working the D.C. circuit. He could not stay in the white hotels, so our Uncle Richard (a man about the town), invited him to stay with us. The next morning he gave everybody free tickets to his show. Our sisters and all of the older family members attended, but the three boys were too young to go.

The highlight of our living at 1201 was the wood and coal business that our grandfather operated in our back yard. He would cut and sell wood for one dollar a basket. He would sell coal for one dollar and fifty cent, a basket. It gave all of us a chance to earn some money making deliveries throughout the neighborhood. Tom built a push cart, which could haul three baskets and he paid us to help him push it. Helen and Grace cut the wood along with our grandfather. Every Saturday night we would line up at the kitchen table for "Pay day." Helen, Grace and Tom always got the most money. Maurice and I got the least.

After our sisters moved to Detroit (except Doris), they would always come home during the summer months for a spring clean-up of 1201. We all pitched in with the painting, repairing and cleaning, since our parents were getting old and needed support. Carpenter Tom, built a white fence around the front yard, and planted flowers and plants all around. I cleaned the carpets and washed the windows. Our sisters painted and decorated each room. Our parents were always pleased at our renovations.

In 2006, there was a Plater/Ware family reunion held in D.C. and the highlight of the reunion was a visit to 1201. The present owner allowed the entire reunion participants to tour the old homestead and take pictures. The memories of life at 1201 was a joy to behold.

## TAKING CHANCES

One of the existing pastimes for us at 1201 was playing the numbers. Of course it was illegal to bet or back the numbers, but the police did not enforce it because it was wide spread in all communities, and secondly, because there were so many more serious crimes being committed at that time. In today's society the lottery is widely used and accepted, however, when we grew up, the comparable system was called "The Numbers." There were numbers runners in every minority community. They provided a betting opportunity for people to secure needed funds for rent and food. The runners would come around every morning to take your bets, and come back every night with your winnings. While the winning lottery numbers are determined by the random pulling of numbers, the daily horse racing results determined the winner for the numbers system. All betters wanted to, "Hit the number" and win. In order to win, they would have to pick any combination of three numbers. If they bet one cents, they could win, one dollar. If they increased it to five cents, they could win two dollars. A ten cents bet would bring them five dollars. A fifty cents bet would bring you eight dollars. Most people would bet one dollar to win thirteen dollars. The numbers players were always concerned about selecting the winning number. When they attended church on Sunday morning where they heard the preacher announce, "Let us sing hymn number 406." "Bless Be the Tide." The next day they would bet on number 406. If someone came to their community with an out-of-state automobile, they would check the license plate numbers and bet on it the next day. They would purchase a "Dream Book" which gave suggested numbers for selected dreams. If you dreamed about birds the night before, you should bet on number 524, horses number 319, cars number 275 boats.

Tom never gambled or bet on the numbers. He used to say I work too hard for my money to gamble it away. Our sister Grace had taught me how to gamble and I would often place bets. I shall never forget the time when both Grace and I persuaded Tom to take a chance and bet on the numbers. He said ok and placed one dollar on a number which was the winner. He received his thirteen dollars that evening and said it's only, "First time luck," and he never played again.

Although Tom was not a gambler, he was smart enough to out wit the opposition in any game of chance. (It was the gambling man who was always looking for a way to beat the odds). Suffice it to say, Tom taught me how to win when we "Pitched pennies to the line." In this game, you had to line up behind a line and pitch your penny to the wall (usually 10 or 12 feet away). Tom said, "Watch and win," he then leaned his body well over the line, keeping his feet behind the line, and then he extended his arm out as far as he could. Finally he lightly tossed his penny to the wall so it would not bounce or spin away. He won every time. When I followed his lead, I won, and he demanded a cut in my winnings. He called it training fees!!

I went to the extreme in gambling, I even ordered a special deck of cards with special eyeglasses that you could read the card from the back without being detected. About this time my praying mother told me that she was worried about my becoming a professional gambler, so she started praying that I would lose, whenever I gambled. I remember saying to her, to please take the hex off of me for one time and allow me to win a substantial amount of money for the last time. My mother said, "No my son, you have to stop gambling." I continued to gamble, and I continued to lose. Finally I gave up my dream for a major win, and my gambling habit was curtailed. Tom never started gambling, he was much better off by not indulging.

***Likewise greet the church that is in their house.***
Romans 16:5

# DON'T EVER GIVE UP

When things go wrong, as they sometimes will
When your road of life seems to go down hill

When your funds are low and your debts are high
When you want to smile but you can only sigh

When problems are overflowing in your cup
Rest if you must, but don't give up

Like a boxer in a 10 round bout
Who drops his guard and is called out

Always hang tough when facing defeat
Show others that you can always take the heat

Sometimes the struggle seems too much to bear
When your blood thickens and there is electricity in your hair

It is then that you learn all too late
That you just fell short at the winning gate

You let fear stop you short of your crown
With a few more yards you can have yelled touchdown

Success is failure turned inside out
Always act like a winner and never leave any doubt

Stick to the fight when you are hardest hit
Shake it off, regroup, use your skill and your wit

Pray, mediate, seek spiritual strength
This source of energy will help you go the length

Fight like a tiger, growl like a pit bull pup
But, no matter what you do, Don't Ever Give Up!!

# II

# The Middle Years

# To Mildred, My 5th Sister

We all remember Mildred as the warm and happy one
She lived with us as we played around the beloved 1201
She taught me how to brush my hair
She made sure that I was never in despair
She washed my face and cut my nails
If I went to jail, she would pay my bail
When Uncle Richard ate his dinner,
      he was always in a happy mood
He never knew that I was hiding under the table
      and that Mildred
Was slipping me some of his food
She made me button up my coat during the freezing D.C. snow
I would go to her saying, "Mildred check me out before I go"
Thomas, Maurice, and I were blessed
      with 4 loving sisters to guide us through life
God gave us Mildred as out 5th sister; she had a heart of gold
She was resourceful and business minded,
      she made money to have and to hold
To know her was to love her, she was quiet,
      tender, she had dignity in her smile
You could detect her mental sharpness, her quick wit, and her
warm humor, if you were ever around her for a while.

# Mother was a Praying Women

To the Memory of Mother Cora Ware

She prayed when we had no food
She prayed when our papa was angry and rude
She prayed when we were depressed and sad
She kept on praying, even when we were glad
I saw her on her knees both night and day
I saw her cry out, "Lord drive old Satan away."
I can still see her praying while washing clothes in the big tub
Her hands were sore from the washboard,
But Jesus helped her while she scrubbed
Sometimes I would hear her speaking in tongues
Then she would break out in a Holy Ghost shout
Still crying Jesus at the top of her lungs
Mother prayed for the pastor, the deacons and the Usher board
When offering time came around she gave all she could afford
I Thank her for being there down through the years
I Thank her for sharing her smiles and your tears
Mother led the noon day prayer service for 49 years
and hundred of prostitutes changed their careers
She was always my friend and my pal, and my buddy
She was there to help me, when the waters got muddy
With her firm love and her helping hand
I'm glad that she helped me to be a, "Total" man
Yes, we didn't always obey your rules
and in later years we paid a price
If only we had listened to you, our health would be better, and
out attitudes would be nice
She made us go to Sunday School, and we had to go to church
Today we all love Jesus, and some are involved in Bible research
She gave us mother with,
and you counseled us to stay away from drugs

It helped us to love our kids,
and now we greet them with a big hug
She never humiliated us in the presence of our friends
She taught us to be tolerant and to repent for all sins
She showed us how to be thrifty and how to save money
She made us see the merits of not abusing sugar,
candy and honey
She made our home the center of happiness and cheer
She helped us play family games and you taught us not to fear
Whenever I stayed out late at night, you would look out the
window, and pace the floor
Your loving concern became very clear, when I rang the bell, and
you always opened the door
Whenever I left home, you would always give me a dime
She reminded me, if I got in trouble to call you anytime
She were always cooking on the big wood stove
She sewed some of out clothes and others had to be wove
If I could hear my mother pray again
If only she could touch me and help relieve my pain
If I could hear her sing, "Amazing Grace How Sweet the Sound,
That Saved a Wretch Like Me."
If I could hear her sing, "My Faith looks up to Thee,
Thou Lamb of Calvary."
Then I could rejoice exceedingly,
because joy bells would be ringing down in my soul
I could be happy telling others about,
"The Greatest Story Ever Told."
Your love will always hold.

# Chapter 6

# 3029 CLINTON STREET
## (A Showcase)

Leader Tom was the first member of the Ware children to purchase his own home. We all marveled at his significant achievement. He and Willemena bought, 3029 Clinton Street, Northeast, and resided there for the next 56 years. It was a showcase home. It was warm and comfortable and well decorated with fine art and paintings. It was a good meeting place for family and friends. Tom and Willemena hosted many parties and social events there.

Fun loving Tom was always the life of the party. He kept a supply of cold beer which he called, "Super Suds," and oysters around for his friends to enjoy while they listened to his huge jazz collection. Years later, he abstained from drinking beer and he went on a strict diet. It helped him because he was never overweight or obese. Additionally, he was better able to survive when his serious illness conditions came down on him later on.

I remember when they invited my forty members ROTC Drill Team to their home for a dinner and after party. We were in D.C. representing our college, N.C.A&T, Greensboro, N.C., at the "National Cherry Blossom College Drill Team Competition" in which we won first place. Tom called his home "The House of Ware" and each day he displayed a colorful flag depicting a holiday or a particular season from his front porch. The garden in his front and back yard was a thing of beauty. He cultivated his flowers and plants all year long.

He could name many varieties of flowers and plants, and he could tell you the type of soil they needed. He could tell which flowers were perennials and when they should be watered and cultivated. He once told me that the state flower for California is the Golden Poppy, for Washington D.C., the state flower is the American Beauty Rose, and for Wisconsin, it is the Violet. The neighbors all marveled at the beauty of 3029 Clinton Street.

It is said that a good gardener has a "green thumb." I believe that Tom's skill in planting plants and flowers makes one believe that he had two green hands. Tom had a unique collection of African paintings, sculptures and artifacts.

## A MUSEUM OF ART

I called his home, "A Treasure Chest," because of the expensive collection. Tom had them environmentally protected with heaters, condensed lighting, and air conditioning units. Tom could give you a detailed version of each painting and painter; he was a student of the arts. He was keenly aware of the value and significance of fine art in high school and he received good grades in painting and mechanical drawing.

Whenever he traveled, he would visit the local art gallery, evaluating and comparing works-of-art. He traveled to Africa and brought back many African paintings. In fact, some of the rare and priceless works of African art that he brought back are currently displayed in the Anacostia Maryland Art Museum. Actually, Tom remodeled 3029 Clinton, to accommodate and display the many works of art collected from all over the world. I once asked him why a person would spend a thousand dollars for a picture to hang on his wall? He answered, "Because of its' intrinsic value, one can consider it an investment." It also gives you a relaxed feeling and some moments of happiness knowing that you are the proud owner of a rare painting! There is at least one African painting, from his house, displayed in the home of each one of his brothers and sisters. I cherish mine and I plan to will it to my son, so it can stay in the Ware family.

## TOGETHER WE STAND

Tom and Willemena enjoyed many happy years together living at 3029 Clinton Street. Actually, they began dating while they were both students at Minor Teachers College. Intellectual Tom was the first member in the Ware family to attend college. It gave the rest of us a renewed desire to further our education.

They had known each other since they were students at Brown Jr. High School. Tom said she was the light of his life and the light was never dimmed. He called her, "Bill." The Bible says, "Whoso findeth a wife, findeth a good thing." Willemena was a good thing for Tom. After graduating from Cardoza High School, Willemena attended Minor Teachers College. She then worked for the National Security Agency (NSA), and the Census Bureau. While at NSA, she was promoted to Supervisor and then Chief of Learning Centers. She was the first black to receive the Instructional Support Award for the year. Tom and Willemena had two boys, Dexter and Kevin. Both boys died of cystic fibrosis at an early age.

## HAVE NO FEAR

As far back as I can remember, my brother Tom was not afraid to do what seemed to be impossible. While he was attending Brown Jr. High School, he was challenged in his woodshop class to draw a blueprint and make a piece of furniture in order to pass the class. Tom decided to make a shoe rack for a wardrobe closet. He was already skilled in printing and drawing, so drawing the blueprint presented no problem. He quickly acquired carpentry skills and he finished the project ahead of his peers. Needless to say, I followed in his foot steps and used the same blueprint, and made a similar shoe rack, one year later when I took the same class.

When he was attending Minor Teachers College, he was faced with the dilemma of attending College full time and working part time, or attending college part time, and working full time. Tom chose to enlist in the Army, so he could get G.I. educational benefits. He was stationed at Fort Leonard Wood, MO, as an infantryman. He earned the Expert Infantryman's Badge and the Good Conduct Medal during his tour. He was honorably discharged in 1951. His first task upon coming home was to marry his lifetime partner, Willemena Boyd.

It is interesting to note that both Tom and I believed that marriage is sacred, and divorce is not an option. We both got married in the same small town, Rockville, Maryland, and we both have enjoyed long successful marriages. Tom and Willemena, fifty-six (56) years, Mollie and me, fifty-four (54) years and counting, I followed Tom's plan of action in celebrating anniversaries. He would always call me and share what they did on their big day. For example, he would say we went horseback riding and had a candlelight dinner afterwards. That same year, I told him, Mollie and I went bicycle riding and had lunch at McDonalds. As the years went by, we were able to afford more. Both of us would always remember our wives on Valentines Day, Mother's Day and of course, Birthdays. Whenever we would take a trip, we would always remember to bring our wives and the kids some token of love when we returned. To our surprise, our wives treated us likewise. They stood by us during the best and worst of times.

As I reflect on Tom's college dilemma, I too was faced with a dilemma. I had followed in Tom's footsteps and started attending Minor Teachers College, but I was intrigued with the girls, social life and partying. After the first semester, the Dean called me in and said, "Mr. Ware, your grades are falling, what are you going to do?" My decision was to join the Air Force, where I remained, for the next twenty-two years. I shall always be grateful for Tom leading the way for me in day to day living.

## WE MUST STOP THEM

Crime was out of control in D.C. The citizens of Clinton Street lived in fear. One of the neighbors said her home was burglarized on a Saturday and on the following Monday, the T.V. that had been stolen from her home was on sale in a yard sale across the street from her. The city police could not respond fast enough to stop the criminals. Irate citizens were afraid to walk the streets night or day because the street gangs patrolled the area selling drugs, robbing people, and harassing women and children. Such was the setting when Tom said, "Enough is enough." (His home had been burglarized twice).

He called for a group of neighbors to meet in his home and urged them to join forces and unite to protect their property. That night, they elected him Captain, as they organized the Woodbridge Neighborhood Watch Program. Armed with whistles, white hats, white arm bands, cell phones and cameras, they patrolled the area in group formation every night. Tom set up a coffee and doughnut stand in front of his home, at his own personal expense. He maintained a direct liaison with the local police. This time the police responded in a timely manner to support the group. Within the next (90) days, the city donated Captain Tom's group, rain gear, flashlights and updated cell phones, shortly thereafter, the criminals relocated and Clinton Street was safe. The group continued to patrol on a limited basis to prevent them from returning. The Washington Post Newspaper wrote an article praising the worthiness of the project and applauding the citizens of Clinton Street. Another victory for Tom.

*"And if your house be worthy, let your peace come upon it, But if it be not worthy let your peace return to you."*
Matthew 10:13

# Chapter 7

# "MR. G.Q"

Sir Thomas was always a fashionable, well dressed clean cut individual. From an early age, he kept his shoes shined and his hair neatly trimmed. He was called "The man of many hats" because of the large variety of hats he wore. He would change his wardrobe two or three times a day. He would start out as a sailor and seafarer, changing later to a jockey/horseman and ending up in his favorite colorful African attire. He called his hats "Fedoras" and he had one for every occasion. He was always matched and well groomed. Tom was sharp and clean, even in his work clothes. He used to tell me, "Little brother, you have to look sharp if you want to be sharp." You could call him, Captain Tom, General Tom, Officer Tom, Attorney Tom, Doctor Tom, or Chief Tom. His wardrobe would always affirm his role.

If Tom had lived in California, he would have been an outstanding actor. He was calm as Denzel Washington, and as witty as Eddie Murphy.

Tom was an excellent dancer. He mastered all of the latest steps. By comparism, I only mastered the slow drag dance.

Our family came up as reserved C.M.E. Methodist and we were accustomed to the word Negro. Tom was the first member of the family to break our tradition as he insisted on us calling him Black. We soon caught on and converted to the more acceptable words, "Black like me!"

## A TREND SETTER

Tom played the super star role as he drove around town in his red convertible Chrysler Le Baron, with his white scarf, designer sunglasses, Barney Olds Field touring cap and black leather gloves. The only thing he missed was a huge dog in the passenger seat. I used to watch him drive off, and I would quietly say, "Go Tom Go."

I forgot to mention that Tom was noted for wearing a handkerchief in his vest pocket and carrying one in his pants pocket to clean his glasses. He wore colorful suspenders and he never wore baggy pants.

I once heard Tom called, "A Gentleman of Culture and Refinement." He was a class ACT in his youth. He kept our bikes and wagons cleaned and well oiled.

Superman Tom was very conscious of physical fitness. He would walk at least one mile every day. He was constantly advising me to lose weight and exercise.

I wish I had heeded his advice. Perhaps I would not be tied to the life sustaining kidney machine that I am on now. He told me about his bout with cancer, and how the doctor gave him only one year to live. Amazingly he beat the odds and lived three years beyond his proposed demise.

By this time in my life, I had reached a low point. I was a low life Air Force degenerate. I was not a good soldier. While home on leave and between party crashing with my running buddies, I went to a revival with my mother. That night I was baptized in Jesus name and saved.

In later years, Tom became acutely aware of having good health. He curtailed using a lot of prescription drugs and substituted them with diet, exercise and healthy living. His favorite exercise was walking. Tom would walk for one mile everyday except on Sunday. He would take his morning walk before breakfast no matter where he was. I remember when he visited me in California; he would encourage me to take a one mile walk with him. I tried and I usually lasted one-half of the mile when I stopped and waited for him to return. He became a strong advocate for nutritious foods.

To my surprise, I did not find out about his cancer until years after his surgery. I had just had surgery for the removal of both my kidneys, when he told me not to worry, because he had had surgery years ago, and it did not slow him down. In fact, Tom hardly ever complained (except about wars and politics). He was always an upbeat individual.

He carried his desires for cleanliness over to his automobiles. He used to say, "Your car should be a clean machine, it runs better when it's clean."

At one time, he bought two Volkswagens, one for himself and one for Willemena. He placed the license plates on Willemena Volkswagen as "B WARE," and the plate on his Volkswagen was, "A WARE."

He went through a series of jobs after his discharge. He was hired as a Correctional Officer at Lorton Reformatory, where he developed arbitration skills that helped him with future employment and management positions. Tom wore uniforms three times during his life, the Army, the Lorton Reformatory, and as an Amtrak Security Officer.

In his Mr. G.Q. style, he wore his uniforms in immaculate manner. He always ironed the creases in his shirts and he kept his shoes highly polished.

## DARK DAYS

At this point and time, I began to notice a change in Tom's behavior. He started acting moody and indifferent, I was hurt when I realized that Tom had changed from his boy-wonder status to that of an angry black man. I kept asking myself and my wife, "What happened to Tom, how can we reconcile in peace as we did years ago, when we fought everyday?"

I remember when he first started to change towards me. For all the years I was in the Air Force, I would always stay at Tom's house when I came home on leave. He would even let me drive his car while there (He and Willemena would share her car). We were very close. One time I called and told him I was coming home and gave him the time and date. When I got to his house, there was a note in the door saying, "Gone shopping, see neighbors next door for the key." Needless to say, there was no key next door and I wondered why was Tom trying to avoid me? I still sent him the usual Birthday and Christmas cards as we had always done, but it really bothered me that we were no longer close brothers?

As I tried to reason what had happened, I could only speculate that I must have caused him to be angry by tactlessly admonishing him as a disgrace to himself, for his drinking habits, and by playing a "holier than thou" role, since I was totally committed to the church, after living a degenerate life.

I realized that emotions can be changed by circumstances, and I wondered if Tom's anger came from frustration, racism, and prejudice, which made him hostile and full of hate. Historically, we note that pent up anger has destroyed many black men and black families, and it should be dealt with as soon as possible.

I started praying, Lord help my brother Tom to be like he used to be! He was there when I needed him, and he helped me! Give me the strength and the wisdom to help him.

There were two significant factors that turned Tom around, one was the constant persuasion from our two wives for us to get along better, and secondly, our sister Bee and our mother praying around the clock for him.

We were all happy when Tom was baptized in Jesus name, and joined the Vermont Avenue Baptist Church. I was glad to hear him call me "Brother" again, and offer to call me and travel with me. Tom was also happy, like the Champion Green Bay Packers football team of the 1960's who had just scored a come back victory, we both adopted their motto, "The Pack is Back." I am pleased to report that we both apologized to each other.

Tom accepted a position as an Amtrak Security Officer where he rose to the rank of Sergeant. He had previously worked at Amtrak before going into the Army. After his promotion to Sergeant, he was promoted to a position of Chief Hearing Officer and finally to an executive position, where he remained until he retired. As the Chief Hearing Officer, he was an expert examiner for employee relations. He was the top administrator for ADA and disabled persons problems. In Employee Relations positions he traveled all over the East Coast to arbitrate cases. Amtrak sent him to Terrell Law School, where he learned how to adjudicate cases in discrimination, sexual harassment cases, unlawful termination, substance abuse, termination and failure to promote. Tom never rendered a quick decision, he always reflected on the case, and gave his decision, thirty days later.

Tom's time of service with Amtrak totaled thirty-four years and upon his retirement, he continued his relations with the company as a consultant. He also enjoyed working as manager of the Sun Gallery Jewelry Store in N.W. Washington D.C.

He received numerous awards for his work. Amtrak employees often called him and thanked him for making an equitable settlement. Our dad, who was a lifetime railroad worker, was very proud of him. Tom was a gifted individual, as pointed out by his pastor, Rev. Wheeler, who preached his Eulogy.

Being saved helped Caretaker Tom to become a Guardian Angel for our brother Maurice, and a trusted strong supporter for me. A friend of ours put it best, when he likened Tom to "Job" in the Bible, a man who had the strength and endurance to go through turmoil and come out a winner.

## THE NEW TOM

I shall never forget how Tom organized our first family prayer breakfast in the back yard of, 1201 "G" Street. He built a wooden cross, which he called, "The Old Rugged Cross," and he used it as the center piece for the ceremony. He called on all of our neighbors and friends to testify about what God had done for them. Tom paid for all the breakfast food. It was a very spiritual service and all of those who attended it, came away rejuvenated and uplifted. When Tom visited us in California, years later, he organized a prayer breakfast in our home. Our neighbors were greatly impressed with the service.

I am grateful for the influence of attending prayer breakfasts and prayer meetings. Moreover, when I was in the Air Force, and I came home on leave, I would always stop at our church for participation in the noon day prayer service which our mother Cora Ware led for forty-nine years. It was a blessing to see cab drivers park their cabs and come into the church for one hour of prayer each day. I saw government workers take their lunch hour in prayer. One day I met a charming young lady, who was a supervisor in the Department of the Navy, taking her lunch break in prayer at the church. I spoke to her and she responded. I knew at that moment, that I wanted to spend the rest of my life with her at my side. I started making marriage plans before I knew her name. After a short courtship, she consented to marry me and we have been together for fifty-four years and counting. We have raised five children, with seven grand children and one great-grand child. I feel that God directed our lives to meet at that prayer service in Washington D.C. I often sing the song, "Just Mollie and Me!"


*Behold an Israelite indeed in whom there is no guile.*
John 1:47

# Chapter 8

# THE WARE AND WARE DEBATES

Both Tom and I were brought up in the church. Our mother, Cora Ware, was a strong woman of God and our oldest sister Bee was a close second. When they put us on their prayer list, they fasted and prayed until the walls of evil came tumbling down. We were both inspired and motivated knowing that we had two prayer warriors supporting us around the clock. Tom eventually joined Vermont Avenue Baptist Church and became a member of their D.C. club, where he spent countless hours helping young people with his time and his money.

I once saw him counsel a young man who was addicted to drugs. Tom stuck with him until he was sober enough to apply for a job. Tom then escorted him there and helped him through the interviewing process. After assuring his potential employer that he would stand behind the young man, he was hired and Tom later went to the jobsite unannounced to make sure of the youngsters success.

Tom used to love to go to the library. He loved to browse and look at the contents of a book before checking it out. He spent a lot of time in the classified section, where he reviewed rare books, public documents and social editions. When he coupled this experience with his use of the internet, it made him a superb scholar.

I often wonder why Tom did not run for a political office, since he was a gifted speaker, a well versed student and a well liked individual. His local city Councilman commended him for delivering votes to his campaign.

## DREAMING

Tom once shared with me some relevant facts about the year 1964. He had fought hard to get D.C. citizens the right to vote for president and it finally happened. For the first time in U.S. History, D.C. citizens could vote for president. Tom and his friends celebrated for more than a month. Other outstanding achievements in 1964 which added to their joy were:

A. Dr. Martin Luther King was awarded the Nobel Peace Prize.
B. The Civil Rights Bill was passed in Congress.
C. Mohammed Ali won the heavyweight boxing championship from Sonny Liston.
D. Massive voter registration drives were launched throughout the South.
E. The 24th Amendment to the constitution was ratified, outlawing the Poll tax
(Which had been used to prevent blacks from voting in the South).
F. In Hollywood, black actor Sydney Poitier won the 1964 Academy Award for best acting in the movie, "Lilies of the Field." He was the first black to ever win this award.

Is it any wonder that Tom and his friends rejoiced and thanked God for sweet victory? They could now vote for the President in D.C. Tom continued to rally the troops and "Get out the vote."

In future elections, those of us who knew Tom, can verify that he never exploited others by showing off his knowledge. Willemena once told me about the time they were at a social event when the question came up about the origin of a rare African painting. Studious Tom knew the answer, but he remained quiet while the others speculated. On the way home she said, "Tom, I know you knew the answer, why didn't you tell them?" Tom said, "Peace be still, my dear. Them that know, don't speak, them that speak, don't know."

## LINCOLN /DOUGLAS DAYS

If I were to sum up all the important things that happened to me and Tom in the seventy-seven years that I knew him, I would have to place the "Ware/And Ware Debates" at the top of the list. Tom was a master debater and I was not far behind. When we debated I always learned from the experience. Sometimes our debates would be heated, and our wives would have to intervene by saying, "Why don't you guys stop long enough to eat dinner?" They never joined in the debate nor did they render their opinion. They just listened and smiled at us.

Tom would always win because he would say, "When I was at" or "I saw" or "I talked to." I usually said, "I heard" or "I read." Tom's experiences were more convincing and relevant most than mine.

For example I remember bragging to him, that I stay up every night playing scrabble on the computer. He answered, "That's good, but that's only a word game. You should stay up like I do and research the internet for information." He went on to say that I should know that former President John F. Kennedy read twenty-five newspapers each day. He read twelve before breakfast. He mastered the art of speed reading. I said, "Tom, how many news papers do you read each day?" He answered, "I read three everyday." I said to myself "WOW." I only read one paper a day and then only certain sections of it. I asked him how many books does he read each month. He responded, at least two.

I then found out that Tom was an avid reader. It should be noted that at his funeral, a literary society set up an annual scholarship in his name to a deserving youth.

In one of our debates, he said, did you know that your State of California was named after a black woman? Her name was Queen Califa. She was a Mythical Warrior Queen who ruled over an island totally populated with black women. No men were allowed on the island except for twenty-four hour maintenance work. If they stayed on the island beyond the twenty-four hour limit, they were executed. He said the internet will tell you that the State of California, with its population of thirty-seven million citizens plus four and one-half million illegal immigrants, its fifty-eight counties, fifty-five Electoral College votes, fifty-three members in the House of Representatives and the sixth largest economy in the world is named after a black woman. On one of my visits to the State Capitol in Sacramento, I noticed a picture of Queen Califa, placed on the walls of the Senate Rules Committee Hearing Room.

Historian Tom had a keen interest in Black History. In one of our political debates, he said did you know that the State of Mississippi had elected a black senator in 1870? His name was Hiram Revels. Actually he was the first black senator elected in the United States.

After I gave him my views on politics, he gave me another lesson on Black History. He said, did you know that in 1872 a black man named Pinckney Pinchback (who was serving as Lt.

Governor for the State of Louisiana), succeeded the Governor who was impeached? He became the first black Governor elected in America.

A young student of history once said to me, "I wish I could spend a whole year in Washington D.C." I would spend many hours visiting the Capitol, the Monument, the Smithsonian Institute and all the famous landmarks of History. I could see them rather than read about them. Tom was blessed to live in D.C. where he had plenty of time to visit and research history. Is it any wonder that he was always well versed when we debated, religion, politics, sports, the war, history, geography, marriage and family life and science.

I never challenged him on the subjects of music or art whenever these subjects surfaced, my inner man would tell me, "Don't go there!!"

Whenever Tom visited me in California, he would greet my friends and co-workers and discuss politics, stocks, sports, religion, art, music or any subject, with anybody, at any place. I remember taking him with me to transact business, Tom started communicating with the Legislators. I was amazed and intrigued with his depth of knowledge about politics, as he conversed with them.

Many of our debates were focused on religion. I had considered myself an astute bible scholar, while he had maintained his desire for reading and studying the bible on a daily basis. I was often embarrassed at how well he could expound on bible scriptures that I thought I was well versed in. Ninety-nine (99) percent of the time he proved to be right.

*Consider what I say, and the Lord,*
*give thee understanding in all things.*
2 Timothy 2:7

# Chapter 9

# NOT QUITE READY FOR PRIME TIME

While Tom was successful in almost everything he attempted to do, the one area where he fell short in sports. Following after him, I too fell short in sports.

While growing up, we both dreamed of running touchdowns on the football field, hitting homeruns, and scoring fifty points in a basketball game. We also looked forward to earning a school letter in high school. We noted how the girls seemed to admire the jocks (sports lettermen) and we wanted to be in that crowd. We both fell below the cut off mark for earning a school letter. On a scale of ten, I would rate Tom at four. I would rate myself at two for sports achievement.

Actually my sports activity was limited at an early age due to a genetic heart murmur. We both tried, and we both made the best of it, as we grew up!

## WE CAN DO IT TOO

As youngsters we had role models in every major sport except baseball and hockey. We looked to Joe Louis in boxing, Jim brown in football, Lou Alcindor in basketball and Jesse Owens in track. Every time they won, we felt like we could be there someday. We could not relate to baseball because prior to 1947, blacks could not play in the major leagues. Of course we did cheer for Satchel Paige in the Negro Baseball League. Leader Tom, cut out the newspaper article and brought it to our hangout, which showed Jackie Robinson being drafted to the Brooklyn Dodgers. He was the first black player in the Major League Baseball and he helped Brooklyn win the Pennant that year. We were grateful to Dodger owner Branch Rickey, for opening the door to black players.

In our hero worship we drank Joe Louis punch, and ate Wheaties as the breakfast of champions. We actually thought that food named after a champion, would make us a champion. Although we didn't follow baseball, we ate Baby Ruth candy bars for the same reason.

In high school we both went out for the track team since we had years of experience running from the police. Tom also went out for football, while I went out for the golf team.

In order to win a school letter, you had to score three or more points anytime during the season. Tom was unable to score any points in football because of his limited playing time. I was unable to score points in golf, because our coach said I hit too many balls into the water and the woods. In track, Tom did a little better he made the team and traveled to the Penn. relays track meet. He was still not good enough to score any points. I also tried out for pole vaulting on the track team. You had to vault fifteen or more feet to qualify for the finals. I could never vault more that twelve feet.

After I went into the Air Force, I joined the boxing team and I quit after an Ape looking heavyweight called Gorilla Jones, knocked me into another world in the first round. I also tried to make the base track team, but I gave up after coming in next to last place each time I ran. So I finally gave up competitive sports.

In football Tom never got much playing time, because he did not weigh enough to be a lineman, and he was not skilled enough to play in the backfield, however, he did play on a community (sandlot) team. The team consisted of young amateur football players who were always matched with a lot of semi-pro players. Tom's coach told them he wanted to scrimmage them against a top team, so they could gain valuable experience. It turned out to be a bone crushing game with a lot of injuries on the field. I was the score keeper and I remember seeing little children running up and down the sidelines and rejoicing saying, "My daddy made that touchdown." They were clearly outmatched. Tom gave up football after that game. In fact we both spent the rest of our lives playing recreational sports.

We both carried Tom's "will to win" into other facets of our life, on the job, in our homes, at social events and in school, in fact, we never gave up.

I was always amazed at the tenacity and strong will that my brother displayed. He seemed to always say, "I will never give up." As our role model, he encouraged Maurice and I to continue fighting for survival and, reaching for the stars. Even though we rarely won in sports, we kept on trying.

In an earlier chapter, the enclosed poem, "Never Give Up," depicts the spirit of this giant of a man. While we gave hero worship to outstanding black sportsmen in our youth, we carried the same feeling to outstanding black sports figures in our adult years, namely:

Track - Wilma Rudolph
Golf - Tiger Woods
Football - Doug Williams

Tennis - Althea Gibson
Boxing - Mohammad Ali
Baseball - Hank Aaron and Bobby Bonds
Basketball – Michael Jordan

To this end, our feelings about black success stories gave us hope for our future. I must say, that while D.C. was highly segregated, not all of the white citizens agreed with the mandated Jim Crow policies. Throughout the city, many friendly white citizens helped us, employed us and encouraged us to get an education.

Although Tom and I were "not quite ready for prime time" in sports, we were blessed to excel in other areas.

> *Though he fall, he shall not be utterly cast down,*
> *for the Lord upholdeth him with his hand.*
> Psalms 37:24

# Chapter 10

# A TRAVELING MAN

While Tom was employed at Amtrak, he was given a train pass for unlimited travel and he made good use of the privilege. He and Willemena took many pleasure and business train trips all over the country. They rarely traveled by air.

Traveler Tom once took a cruise with his church to Brazil, South America. There, he was welcomed like an African Chief which pleased him. He also took numerous trips to Bermuda and the Bahamas. Traveling in America was routine for the Wares. They would go shopping in New York and Chicago, and return home with a large array of clothes, jewelry, and art.

They traveled to Africa and brought back some Kente cloth (worn by African Chiefs), some copper bracelets which are supposed to lower your blood pressure (I still sleep with mine each night). They also visited the Louvre in Paris (an 18th Century Royal Palace). While in Europe, they made short visits to all of the surrounding countries, (i.e.) Holland, Sweden, Belgium and Germany.

Whenever they visited your home, they would respect you as the host. They would accompany you to your church, and help you clean your swimming pool, or wash your car. My wife was pleased because they would always help wash the dishes and prepare the meals. It is said that the Ware's took two trips each month, one for business, and the other for pleasure and shopping.

Tom once said that he had experienced all types of transportation, ships, cars, trains, bicycles, boats, horses and airplanes. He said I have not traveled in a submarine or spaceship, but he wanted to. He was a courageous man.

## WELCOME TOM

In 1999, my wife Mollie helped me to plan a heart warming welcome to Tom and Willemena, as they visited us in Sacramento, California. We wanted them to experience our West Coast Culture. Mollie had gathered many of our friends and neighbors at the train station with a huge sign saying, "Welcome To California." There were little kids singing and waving banners, we all had on straw hats. As he walked into my house, his first words were, "I would like to arrange a prayer breakfast in your backyard." He then built a wooden cross for the altar, and he led the prayer breakfast, he was a blessing to our home.

Tom's favorite nieces and nephews lived in Detroit, so he would travel there at least once a month. We always had a close kinship to them since they had lived with us for a time at, 1201 "G" Street. There was Bernard Lamar whom we called Butch, and Morris whom we called Porky. The girls were Doris, whom we called Ronnie, and Janice who was just like her mother Helen, and then the baby, Mary, who looked like our Aunt Ella. They were all well trained, sweet and respectable kids. Helen insisted on it. We were called, Uncle Thomas, Uncle Maurice and Uncle Junior. Even though I am now seventy-six years old, they still call me Uncle Junior. When they lived with us at 1201 years ago, I can remember walking from 1201 "G" Street (approx. 16 blocks) to buy diapers for Porky (the baby at that time). In recent years, Tom traveled with the Detroit group to North Carolina, for a combined family vacation. On another occasion, the group traveled to visit us in California. It was like a mini family reunion to have all of them with us.

Tom and Willemena would often travel to Chicago to spend quality time with a spectacularly young lady named Sherby Miller whom they adopted as their god-daughter. They did not have to help her in the traditional god-parent role, because she had already achieved outstanding success in business and education. Another Detroit niece that Tom helped was the daughter of our sister Bee, Loveline Toombs. Tom also shared his love for our nieces and nephews in Washington D.C. by providing surrogate father duties with them! He was there when they had significant life problems. Included in this group were the off springs of our sister Doris, the warm and active Claudine McLaughlin Barnes and Derrick McLaughlin. The loving and aggressive children of our sister Grace, Yvonne Ware-Gaston, Dennis Johnson, Anthony and David Johnson. Tom was also very helpful to Yvonne's son, Harold (Red) Ware. Our friendly Brother-in-law, Jim Johnson, also stood in the gap for the Ware children in time of need. I was only available to help, when I came home on leave from the Air Force. But, Tom checked on the D.C. group everyday. Actually, he was supportive of the children and children's children of all of our relatives. They could count on "Uncle Tom" to bail them out and to help them with their finances.

The joy of railroading is imbedded in the hearts and minds of all the Ware family one could say that trains are in our blood stream, and there is a train in our future! From the early Ware days when the Ware kids had to walk two miles to take our father his lunch at the Union Station (where he worked, loading trains) to the later years when we traveled by train for pure joy and relaxation, trains have been a part of us. Is it any wonder that Tom spent thirty-four years working around trains? I travel via train wherever I can.

As kids we kept on our traveling shoes and we were always ready to travel. Tom used to always sing, "I'm Working on the Railroad all the Live Long Day." I still sing, "I'm Going Home on the Morning Train."

## THERE IS A TRAIN IN YOUR FUTURE

We all love trains. I can remember wanted to follow Tom, (who was working at Amtrak) so I took and passed the Railroad Mail Clerk Examination. I would have been assigned to a traveling train as a mail sorter; unfortunately the increased efficiency of air mail service curtailed the need for forwarding mail via train. So I had to seek other employment.

Tom and I have spent countless hours visiting the California Railroad Museum here in Sacramento. In fact, Tom donated some early Amtrak memorabilia to the Museum for display.

Whenever Tom would travel on an Amtrak train, the Red Caps would never accept a tip from him. They remembered the job he had done for them while he was on the Executive Amtrak Board, and the way he helped them as a Hearing Officer for Amtrak and they wanted to express their appreciation. He was always the recipient of gratitude from railroad employees. God gave Tom a special anointing for helping and caring for others. I guess we could call it a "Rare Ware" trait because all of our sisters and myself had the same gift for helping others.

Tom's love for trains extended beyond Amtrak, and American Railroading. He was also intrigued with the trains in foreign countries. He shared stories about the fast moving (bullet) trains in Japan which were noted for on/time departures and arrivals. In fact, if a Japanese train did not arrive in time, it was considered an insult to the Emperor, and the Engineer was punished.

Moreover, he was fascinated with European trains that used high quality silverware and the finest glass and linen napkins in their dining cars.

He had a profound interest in the via/rail Canada Railroad, and he often talked about exploring North America and viewing the highest snow covered peaks of the Canadian Rockies, as well as the rushing tides of the Atlantic Ocean.

My interest in Canadian railroading was sparked when we planned a joint trip from Vancouver Canada to Toronto/Windsor Canada. Tom had to cancel out; however, I finally took the trip across Canada via rail. It proved to be an enjoyable and inspirational trip.

Mollie and I have traveled to all fifty states and 17 foreign countries and we can certainly agree with Tom that traveling broadens your horizon and peaks your learning. He once told me that, when he travels he is better able to plan, think, meditate, and pray.

*"Yea though I walk through the"*
*Valley of the shadow of death, I will fear no evil.*
Psalms 23:4

# III

# On Being a Father

# BEE

*"Our Beloved First Sister"*

You were the first born in our family,
Papa H called you Brewer Lee.

You were the first person to baby sit me as a child,
You taught me how to walk and you taught me how to smile.

You were the first of the children to get a full time job,
You told us that we did not have to steal
and we should never go out to rob.

From your earnings you brought us food
and clothes during the depression years.
You taught us how to love and you taught us how to pray,
You were the family role model and we followed you everyday.

You taught us how to work and play and stay in unity,
You taught us the real meaning of, "We Are Family."

You helped us with our homework
and you walked with us to school.
You taught us not to lie and cheat, but to live by the golden rule.

You protected us and fought for us sometimes all day long,
I can still hear you saying to our enemies,
"This is my brother, right or wrong."

You were the first to lead our family through the pit falls of life,
You were the first one to guide us through the turmoil of
adversity and strife.

You were the first member of the family
to travel away from home,
When you left D.C. for Detroit, you actually traveled alone.

You hit the ground running 80 years ago,
You were always fair with everyone,
the big, the little, the high and the low.

You were the first one in the family to lead us into holiness,
From your giant step forward 125 souls have been blessed.

You were the first in many areas.
You were the first, right from the start.
As for me and my house, we will always love you.
You will always be first in my heart.

# FORTY INSPIRATIONAL SAYINGS

## Dedicated to All Fathers

1.  And the king was much moved. And went up to the chamber over the gate. And wept: And as he went, thus he said. O my son Absalom. my son. my son Absalom! Would God I had died for thee, O Absalom. my son. my son!
    II Samuel 18:33

2.  The greatest thing a father can do for his children is to love their mother.
    J. McDowell

3.  Children need love, especially when they don't deserve it.

4.  The strongest evidence of love is sacrifice.
    C. Fry

5.  A child is not likely to find a father in God unless he finds something of God in his father.
    G. Wheeler

6.  You can not teach a child to take care of himself, unless you let him try. He will make mistakes, and out of these mistakes he will gain wisdom.
    H. Beecher

7.  Train your child in the way in which you know you should have gone.
    C. Spurgeon

8. The best way to teach character is to practice it around the house.

9. Praise your children openly, reprove them secretly.
   W. Cecil

10. The best thing you can give your children next to good habits. Are good memories.
    S. Harris

11. Lord, give me a son whose heart is clear, whose goals are high. One who will reach into the future, yet never forget the past.
    O. McArther

12. A man who thinks that helping with the dishes is beneath him, will also think that helping with the baby is beneath him, and he will not be a successful father.
    E. Roosevelt

13. It may be hard on some fathers not to have a son, but it is harder on a boy not to have a father.
    S. Gilbert

14. The most effective thing that we can do for our children is to pray for them.
    A. Evens

15. A father should never make distinctions between his children.
    Uknown

16. If you tell your children the truth, you don't have to remember what you said.

17. An easy way to make your children miserable is to satisfy all of their demands.
W. Holmes

18. Fathers will spend their earnings on worldly goods, and fail to take care of family needs and survival.

19. Like Father, like son. Every good tree makes good fruit.
W. Langford

20. Govern your family as you would cook fish. Very Gently!
Uknown

21. Words have an awesome impact, the impressions made by a fathers voice can set in motion, a negative trend for life.
G. McDonald

22. A father who comes home from a hard days work, is uplifted when his kids greet him with two magic words, "Hi dad".

23. I could never be angry with my father, he took me hunting and fishing, he spent a  lot of time with me.
J. Dobson

24. A man's children and garden reflect the amount of weeding done during the growing season.

25. The first duty of a father's love is to listen!
P. Tillick

26. Many a man spanks his children for things his own father should have spanked him for.
P Marquis

27. Rarely does a child die from getting to much praise, but once every minute a child dies on the inside, for lack of it.
C. Osbourne

28. Good fathers monopolize the listening. Poor fathers monopolize the talking.
D. Scharze

29. There is no greater vocation for a man than fathering.
J. Thorpe

30. You don't have to be a roaring lion to manage your house.

31. A father's words are like a thermostat that sets the temperature in the house.
P. Lewis

32. Every father is the family role model, whether he wants the job or not.
D. Rodney

33. Children are like clocks, they must be allowed to run.
J. Dobson

34. If you keep telling your son something is wrong with him, he will soon believe it. Instead, try telling him what's right with him.
J. Anderson

35. Its better to bind your child to you by a feeling of respect, and gentleness, rather than fear.
T. Rence

36. The superior man stands erect by bending down. He rises by lifting others up.
R. Ingersoll

37. Nothing I have ever done, has given me more pleasure and reward than being a father to my children.
B. Cosby

38. It takes time to be a good father, it takes effort, trying, failing, and trying again.
T. Hansel

39. Among all the abuses of the world, there is none worse tan negligent fathers.
S. Gauzo

40. To become a father is not hard; to be a father is hard.
W. Busch

# TESTIMONIAL

## BRIAN'S STORY

*A father's love can give us a deep, inner sense of being valued and loved. It's absense can haunt us all our lives.*

I was just twelve when my boy Scout troop planned a father-son campout. I was thrilled and could hardly wait to rush home and give my father all the information. I wanted so much to show him all I'd learned in scouting, and I was so proud when he said he'd go with me.

The Friday of the campout finally came, and I had all my gear out on the porch, ready to stuff it in the car the moment he arrived. We were to meet at the local school at 5:00pm and car pool to the campground.

But dad didn't get home from work until 7:00pm. I was frantic, but he explained how things had gone wrong at work and told me not to worry, we could still get up first thing in the morning and join the others. After all, we had a map. I was disappointed, of course, but decided to just make the best of it.

First thing in the morning, I was up and had everything in the car while it was still getting light, all ready for us to catch up with my friends and their fathers at the campground. He had said we'd leave around 7:00am, and I was ready a half hour before that. But he never came out of his room until9:00am.

When he saw me standing out front with the camping gear, he finally explained that he had a bad back and couldn't sleep on the ground. He hoped I would understand and that I'd be a "big boy" about it... but could I please get my things out of his car, because he had several commitments he had to keep.

Just about the hardest thing I've done was to go to the car and take out my sleeping bag, cooking stove, pup tent, and supplies. And then, while I was putting my stuff away in the storage shed and he thought I couldn't see. I watched my father carry his golf clubs out and throw them in the his trunk and drive away to keep his "commitment" That's when I realized my dad never meant to go with me to the campout.

**I didn't matter to him, but his golfing buddies did.**

# BLACK HISTORY

REVELS, Hiram Rhodes, (1827 -1901)

Senate Years of Service: 1870-1871
Party: Republican

*Library of Congress*

REVELS, Hiram Rhodes, a Senator from Mississippi; born in Fayetteville, Cumberland County, N.C., on September 27,1827; attended various schools, seminaries, and Knox College, Galesburg, 111.; barber; ordained a minister in the African Methodist Episcopal Church at Baltimore, Md., in 1845; carried on religious work in Indiana, Illinois, Kansas, Kentucky, Tennessee, and Missouri; accepted a pastorate in Baltimore, Md., in 1860; at the outbreak of the Civil War assisted in recruiting two regiments of African American troops in Maryland; served in Vicksburg, Miss., as chaplain of a Negro regiment and organized African American churches in that State; established a school for freedmen in St. Louis, Mo., in 1863; settled in Natchez, Miss., in 1866; elected alderman in 1868; member, State senate 1870; elected as a Republican to the United States Senate; presented his credentials upon the readmission of Mississippi to representation on February 23, 1870; took the oath of office on February 25, 1870, after the Senate resolved a challenge to his credentials, and served from February 23, 1870 until March 3, 1871; first African American Senator; secretary of State ad interim of Mississippi in 1873; president of the Alcorn Agricultural College, Rodney, Miss., 1876-1882; moved to Holly Springs, Marshall County, Miss., and continued his religious work; died in Aberdeen, Miss., January 16, 1901; interment in Hill Crest Cemetery, Holly Springs, Miss.

# BLACK HISTORY

Pinckney Pinchback, officer and politican...

May 10
"On this date we mark the birth of Pinckney Benton Stewart Pinchback. He was a Black Civil War officer and politician.

Born in Macon, GA in 1837, Pinchback began supporting his family at twelve after his father died. They had moved to Cincinnati, where he found work as a cabin boy. When the Civil War broke out he went to New Orleans and in 1863, was able to join the Union National Guard, He raised and commanded an entire company in a month. The issue of racism held true though, the New Orleans area was very cruel and he was not given his officers commission because he was Black.

After the war Pinchback entered politics in Louisiana. In 1872 when Governor Henry Clay Warmoth was impeached, Pinchback, who had been Lieutenant Governor, succeeded him, serving for over a year, and thus became the first black governor in America.

Pinckney Pinchback earned a Law degree from Straight University in New Orleans and was admitted to the states Bar in 1886. He moved to Washington D.C. and in 1890 organized the American Citizens Equal Rights Association, traveling extensively throughout the country forming local branches. Pinckney Benton Stewart Pinchback died in 1921.

# MILLION MAN MARCH AD

## CALLING ALL MEN
## TO
## A HOLY DAY FOR
## AFRICAN AMERICANS

Join The

## *MILLION MAN MARCH*

Let's Turn Back To GOD
Let's Turn to each other in Unity
Let's Stop Killing Each Other
Let's Take Responsibility For Our Families
Let's Rebuild Our Communities

## SIGN UP TODAY!!

Call (202)726-1111 or (202) 678-8822
For more Information


Rev. Willie F. Wilson, Pastor
Union Temple Baptist Church- Local Coordinator
Dr. Ben Chavis-National Coordinator
Minister Louis Farrakhan-Visionary

# Chapter 11

# LET US BREAK BREAD TOGETHER

My brother was a firm believer in the motto, "If you can't beat them, join them." He had no problem breaking bread with others. No one was a stranger to him. He would join a group and before long, work his way up to be its leader. Tom was always reaching for the stars.

The organizations that he belonged to included the Washington Railroad Retirement Club, a group of retired railroad workers. The Sportsman Association, (comprised of a group of ardent sports fans who compared notes on sports activities), the "R.D. Bunch," which was a group of die-hard Redskin/Dallas fans who kept the rivalry alive between the two teams. They celebrated for a solid month when black quarterback Doug Williams led the Washington Redskins to a super bowl victory in 1988. Doug was the first black quarterback to start, and win a super bowl. He was voted M.V.P, as he threw four touchdowns and beat the Denver Broncos 42-10. He is now the head football coach at Grambling University. Another proud group that Tom joined, and moderated was, "The Group of Fellows," who met every Monday night. This fun group was restricted to men only. They shared information on people, places, and things, at each meeting.

## SPEAK THE TRUTH

One of their basic rules for the group was that a speaker must be able to confirm his facts. Tom was an expert at remembering facts, and his contributions to the group were greatly accepted. He was blessed with many years of experience with our "G" Street corner gang, as we spent countless hours debating issues. Tom would carry newspaper clippings in his pockets to confirm his statements

## SAD TIME

Of all the groups that Tom joined, there was one that made him very unhappy. It was a Greek fraternity called Epsilon. This college organization required its members to achieve high academic skills, complete a test passing phase, social grace phase and a hazing phase, for final acceptance to their ranks. Tom breezed through the test passing phase with flying colors. He told how each member was required to memorize two questions and the correct answer from their final exam, in each class they attended. The questions and answers were then filed in the fraternity office for future use. Specifically, it was noted that a Sociology 101 Professor would give the same final exam for three years before changing it. Tom scored high points for making constructive suggestions to his professors, which pleased his classmates. For example, his history professor assigned the class to read ten books and prepare a book report on one of the ten books. Tom suggested that each student should read one book and form small study groups to discuss what they had read. They would still do their one book report, but they would have a working knowledge of ten books instead of one book.

Tom had no problem with the social grace requirement, but he fell short on completing the hazing phase.

One of the few times I ever saw my brother Tom, confused, bitter and hurt, was when he shared with me, his ordeal with the Epsilon Fraternity, where the Dean of Pledges had blindfolded him and drove him to Rock Creek Park, and members of the group beat him, and led him into the woods, and told him to find his way back to the starting point alone. To make matter worse, it was a dark, cold, and wet night. Tom stumbled and fell in an icy creek trying to get out of the woods. He was disoriented and angry and he kept saying, "Why is all this necessary?" He did not get back to the campus until the next day, where he resigned from the pledge program and never returned to any Epsilon meetings.

Later in life, he joined the church and social clubs, always expressing his concern for mingling with the masses.

His concern for the health and welfare of others caused him to be appointed caretaker and guardian for our brother Maurice. He made sure that Maurice was properly medicated and comfortable. On one occasion, I brought Maurice to California to live with me, but he was very unhappy out here. He rejoiced when Tom flew here to take him back to D.C.

## THERE IS MUSIC IN THE AIR

Tom was always inclined to music. He could play the bass fiddle, beat drums and master the xylophone. He was also blessed with a strong tenor voice. He was fascinated with jazz and he attended concerts and festivals at every opportunity.

I remember attending clubs where he played with a jazz Quartet in D.C. The Quartet leader was Chris Holmes, who played alto sax and emulated the late Illinois Jaquett, by jumping on and off the tables while playing. Tom played the base fiddle and the xylophone. He was noted for turning the base fiddle around while playing it.

Then there was George Chisley, who would stand up and dance while playing the piano. And finally, there was James Woods, who would yell out, "Give the drummer some," while beating the drums. James would then do a long solo drum beating demonstration. The Quartet was very popular in Northeast D.C. during the 1940's. Tom was also a member of HR-57, a jazz enthusiast group, as well as the Fisher Middleton Jazz Foundation. The group of sophisticated jazz critics were highly respected. If you traveled in Tom's car, or visited his home, you could always hear soft contemporary music playing around you.

Tom was the only member of the Ware family who could play a musical instrument. As a youngster, he was always singing and tapping out music, and dancing, so much so, until our grandfather once told our mother, "That boy has music in his bones, you should give him music lessons." Of course our parents could not afford to give us music lessons, so Tom had to learn through trial and error. It was a successful venture for him, because he became a reliable musician.

During his high school years, he beat the base drum in the ROTC Military Band. I was honored, that he let me carry the huge bass drum while he played it, as we marched down Pennsylvania Avenue during Presidential Inaugural Parades.

I shall always remember Tom, as the happy singing individual, who was ready to break bread, sing, and drink beer and wine with kings, presidents and leaders as well as ordinary people.

During the 1930's, there were no TV's, DVD's or CD's in our homes. In fact, we had two small battery operated radio's that stayed on around the clock. There was one upstairs and one downstairs. There were no telephones, refrigerators or washing machines, because there was no electricity. We used the old fashioned wash tub to wash clothes, and we used kerosene lamps to get through the dark nights. Of course we used wood and coal for cooking and heating. Things got better for us by the time I was five years old (so I'm told). In 1935 we got our first telephone and we had electric power for updated living. Since our granddad had a wood/coal business in our back yard, we had an endless supply of fuel.

In our younger years, we all listened to the two radios in our house for our entertainment. The popular radio programs such as, "The Green Hornet, Walter Winchell Gabriel Heater, The Shadow Knows, and Amos and Andy," consumed most of our time, but Tom, my mother, our sister Bee, and myself, all enjoyed a program called, "The Sheep and the Goats." This musical program played gospel records which represented the sheep and followed with the playing of a popular worldly record which represented the Goats. In our own minds we felt a sense of, "Doing the right thing," if we favored the Sheep records and if we could feel a spiritual movement within us, as we sang along with the sheep music, we felt it was pleasing to God. The sponsors for the Goat music were beer and alcohol distributors. Churches and social groups sponsored the sheep programs. It was obvious to whom each group was catering to!!

I can't help but feel that much of Tom's success in life was attributed to his outgoing personality, and his love for people.

One can see that he broke bread and joined many organizations including, the Boy Scouts and Jr. Elks, in his strong political ties. He was always encouraging others to join, vote, and support worthy causes. I always wanted to be just like my brother.

> *"And they continued steadfastly, in the Apostles"*
> *Doctrine, and fellowship, and in breaking bread.*
> Acts 2:42

# Chapter 12

# A FATHER'S LOVE

When our dad passed away in 1977, he left Tom with his railroad stop watch, he left Maurice with his pass and I.D., and he left me with a pair of his work overalls. This was his way of giving us symbols to show us that we must always work and care for our families. He hated the term, "Dead beat dad." After 30 years, I still have the overalls which I will leave to my only begotten son Ted in whom I am well pleased.

Tom was blessed to have two boys, however, God took them home at an early age. He continued to show his love for children by giving guidance and counsel to parents. He is the god-parent to many children. As I reflect on fatherhood, I can never forget an incident that I witnessed while working as Ombudsman for the California Department of Corrections. My job was to investigate and resolve problems for staff and inmates. The Department had just changed its policy to house three inmates in a cell designed for two (due to overcrowding). We had started getting complaints about the crowded conditions and I had to check it out. To my surprise the first overcrowded cell I visited was housed with a father and his two sons. The father remorsefully explained to me that he had trained his two sons (at an early age) how to rob, steal, cheat and commit crime. They were all apprehended while robbing a liquor store. The father was driving the get away car. At their trial, the judge sentenced them to twenty years each, and the Department of Corrections allowed them to be housed together. As I interviewed them, I kept thinking how tragic it was for the mother and wife in that family. She had to visit her husband and two sons in the same cell for the same crime. For the next (20) years.

## A REAL FATHER

In another chapter of this book, there are forty inspirational sayings which some fathers keep beside their night stand, where they read one saying each night at bedtime while they meditate on it before retiring.

For the past 5 years (at Tom's suggestion), I have led a father/son ministry at my church. This surrogate father program takes young boys in field trips, give them counseling, leading them in competitive sports and teaching them spiritual values as well as how to respect women and girls. The program is highlighted with a ceremony called, "The Making of a Man-Child." It has had great success over the years.

As we matured, Tom and I talked about how we would raise our children after marriage. We both wanted to give our kids more than what we had in life, but yet, we wanted to maintain the same Ware tradition of love, caring and sharing.

I remember a personal incident regarding child discipline that caused me to repent and change my thoughts on child rearing. I had always thought that a parent should keep his belt or a stick or ironing cord handy to beat his children when they were out of line! I later realized that there is a point in your child's growth that you have to lay aside the belt and the beatings and use other methods of discipline. Although I still believe in spanking little toddlers, the incident that changed me happened in Ramstien Germany in

1968 (we were in the Air Force at that time). I remember telling my children to stay away from the woods located a short distance from our backyard. I had been told that animals and predators were in the woods and that some children who went into those woods were never seen again! The area was posted with signs and a small fence; however, some kids climbed over the fence and did not heed the "DO NOT ENTER" signs.

My daughter Angela (age nine), at the time was one of those disobedient kids. I came home one day and I noticed that she was coming out of the woods. I went into a rage, took off my belt, ran out to the woods and started beating her! As I yelled, "I told you to stay out of the woods," my wife Mollie ran out behind me and pulled me away from her as she was crying and scared. I later realized that for a few minutes I had lost consciousness of what I was doing. My rage had changed me into something I did not want to be! I repented when I saw the scars on her legs weeks later. I was hurt knowing that I had put the scars there and I said, "Was it worth all this, to teach her a lesson?" Finally I prayed Lord Jesus, please help me to raise and discipline my children without the potential for violence. Keep my mind and thoughts on love and help me to remain firm but not fanatic. From that day forward. I never beat my children again. I thank God for guiding me over the years.

Strangely enough, in 1978, I saw the consequence of what happens when a parent is mean and abusive to his children. I was on the California Youthful Offender Parole Board and we had a young 13 year old girl before us who had just murdered her entire family. One morning her abusive father yelled upstairs for her to come down to breakfast (he insisted on the whole family eating their meals together). This particular morning the little girl was depressed and hurt. She did not respond to him, so he threatened to come up stairs and beat her if she did not come down now! Finally the little girl started downstairs with her hands behind her (while he was calling her, she was looking in his closet where he kept his guns). When she reached the table she pointed the gun at her father and shot him. She then emptied the gun chamber as she shot her mother, her brother, her sister and the family dog. She then called 911 and said, "I just killed my family. My daddy was mean to me." Our job on the board was to assess how long a juvenile offender should be incarcerated and then to parole them if we felt they were ready to return to society. As we interviewed her, her answer to all of our questions was, "My daddy was mean to me." We finally sentenced her to 25 years which was the longest youth sentence ever given to a youngster, up to that time. We also ordered her to psychiatric intervention. As I looked at her, I thought about her dad, my mind flashed back to my incident ten years before, and I said, "There, but by grace of God go I."

In the book of 2 Samuel, we find that Absolum (Father of Peace) is the son of David. As the story goes, Absolum slew his half brother Amnon for defiling his sister, Tamar. He fled the scene afterwards. Joab who was the commander of David's army hired a woman of Tekoah to appear before David and seek justice. In his wisdom, David detected that Joab was behind the request, however, he also noted strong public opinion supporting her. David then commissioned Joab to bring Absolum back to Jerusalem. At first David would not admit Absolum, but after two years, David accepted him (2 Samuel 14:33). Absolum then set his sights on becoming King, although in 2 Samuel 7:12, it points out that the throne was pledged to another. He gained the favor of the people, raised a large army and rebelled against David. However, David's army defeated him. As he was retreating, Joab killed Absolum in B.C. 1023. Although David had ordered his life be sparred. 2 Samuel 18:9-17, gives an account of Absolums death and burial.

2 Samuel 18:33, gives a touching scenario of David mourning over the death of his son Absolum. Showing a fathers love for his son. The father was reconnected to his son.

In his book on Fatherhood, Bill Cosby gives a down to earth reality check on what it means to be a father. He raised five children and he talks about the rewards and consequences. He refers to the baffling question of a man's decision to father a child, stating, writers have said, the reason to have children is to give your self immortality." You want your name carried on after you are gone, but sometimes your children can be so bad until you don't want them to be associated with your name. He has gone around the country asking people, "Why did you have your children, and he gives the following list of replies to the question:

A. Because I wanted someone to carry on the family name
B. Because a child will be an enduring refection of myself
C. Because I wanted someone to look after me in my old age

He says, to be a successful father, you have to show a lot of love and have a lot of luck.

There is the true story about a father who wanted to be a lawyer. He graduated from law school and took the bar exam fifty-two times (record for California) over a twenty-six year period. He finally passed it. Meanwhile he put his son through law school and the son passed the bar the first time out. The son opened up a law firm and hired his father to practice in his firm. This true to life story affirms the belief that a father/son relationship can be binding. I encourage all fathers to reunite and bind yourself with your son.

Fathers provoke not your children. The book of Ephesians 6:14, tells fathers to provoke not your children to wrath. Wrath is created by sin. God wants us to nurture our children, train them and love them. Teach them to love the Lord. If we study the history of serial killers, we find that most of them had abusive parents.

## THE PRODIGAL SON RETURNS HOME

In the book of Luke 15:12-13, the younger son of his family gathered up all his belongings and went into the far country where he wasted all his money and goods on riotous living. The word "prodigal" means, "One who spends money lavishly and foolishly!" When the day of reasoning came, the son found himself living in a pigpen, feeding the swine. He then realized that his father was well off and that he treated servants better than he was living, so he decided to go back home. The father knew that his son would be coming back and he was waiting for him to return. As he saw him, he ran to him and hugged him. It is noted that under Mosaic Law, the father could have taken the son to the Elders "as a disobedient son" and he could have been stoned to death. But he had compassion and he welcomed his son home. The son said, "Father I have sinned against heaven, and I am not worthy to be called your son," but the father gave him the finest robe, a ring and some shoes, and they had a great feast. The son was reconnected to his father!

I am happy to note that black fathers are taking more responsibility for their families and are not abandoning their children. In the past, more than 80% of all black children were living without a father present in the home. Further statistics revealed in a recent Ebony Magazine article entitled, "The New Black Father," that children raised without their dads are more prone to be jailed, obese, lack of self esteem and have sub-standard education. An alarming number of black fathers are incarcerated. Fortunately, they participate in jail house programs in how to mentor their children.

It has been said that good father's are like strong teeth, often taken for granted while they are here and missed when they are gone.

In the testimonial, "Brian's Story," Brian felt like his father did not love him. He started to hate his father and all mankind. He eventually turned to a life of crime, and he ended up in prison for the rest of his life. The father could have sparred his son's fate by showing more love and caring for his son at an early age.


*"I will be to him, a father, and he shall be to me a son."*
Hebrews 1:5

# IV

## The Twilight Years

# THROUGH THE YEARS

*To My Wife Mollie on the Occasion of*
*Our 35th Wedding Anniversary*

*Dear Mollie,*

Thank you for standing with me for 35 years.
Forgive me for all the hard times I caused you,
all the suffering and, all the tears.

Thank you for actually saving my life,
by helping me to seek medical attention
and proving that you are a wonderful wife.

Remember how you kept saying,
*"Honey please see a doctor, you look tired, and you look sick."*
Meanwhile the swelling around my eyes
kept getting puffy and thick.

But I said I don't need to see them, they are losers
and I am a winner.
My, was I surprised,
whey you invited the doctor to our house for dinner!!

He took one look at me and said,
*"Sgt. you need to be in a hospital bed.*
*If I don't send you right away, in 6 months you will be dead!"*

So Mollie for this and other reasons
I know that you were meant for me.
I loved you then, and I love you now
and I will love you throughout all eternity!

I fell in love with your picture
while I was in the Air Force in 1951.
I carried it around and gazed at it so much,
until the guys thought I was deaf and dumb.

Yes, you were a beautiful lady and you weighed only 98 pounds.
Back then, I tipped the scales at 140,
but now papa has gotten a little round.

When I met you, I was tired of running around
and I wanted to change my life.
I took one look into your eyes and your soul,
I knew right then, that I want this lady to be my wife.

God blessed us to get saved in the same revival.
Working for the Lord increased our chances for survival.

Remember when we were dating,
and I had just brought a 52 Chevy!
One night you refused to let me take you home after service.
You said my passenger load was too heavy.

Actually, I was just taking three young ladies home from church,
And after dropping them off, I thought we could have some
academic/romantic research!!
I had reserved you a front seat, right next to me,
And I was awaiting your presence,
And the sweet aroma of your perfume with great anxiety.

It was then that I realized that you have class and you have style!
As you looked at me with a great big smile,
You said, *"James be a good Christian, and take the girls home,*
*And when you are finished and all alone, call me on the telephone."*

I remember saying, I can't wait any longer,

*"Mollie will you marry me?"*
You waited three long days before you said,
*"Yes, provided my parents will agree."*

Our wedding took place on a Rockville, MD. farm,
and it left much to be desired,
It took us 35 years to do it again,
although we both will soon be retired.

Remember how we both agreed
to never argue in front of our kids?
Actually there were times
when our anger reached the near boiling point,
And we were ready to separate
and put all of our belongings up for bids.

Thank God our prayers helped us to control our emotions.
I would leave the house and go out for a walk or a jog,
Sometimes you would join me, as we both walked the dog!

And then there was the time,
when we said good bye to your mom and dad.
Somehow your father was not very happy in fact,
he seemed a little sad.

He knew that I was taking his little girl,
And that the Air Force would be taking us all over the world.

I shall never forget his parting words to me,
As we prayed and said good-bye, and we left Washington D.C.

He said, "Son, we brought Mollie up in a holy home and we did
not argue and we did not fuss. Now, if you can't treat her like we
did, you bring her right back to us!!

How much do I love you? Let me count the ways.
It is hard to explain just how I feel,
so I have to measure it in time and days.

Mollie, for 420 months you have endured our marriage.
For 1820 weeks, you took care of the kids
and pushed the baby carriage.
For 12,775 days, you listened to my complaints.
A few times, during the 1 million, 706 thousand, 600 hours,
you practiced passive restraint.

And finally for 1 Billion, 100 million, 706 thousand 100 seconds,
You followed God's word, and you always remained.

Through the years, I have loved you.
Through the years, I have cared.
Through the years I have protected you.
Through the years I have shared.


As we pause to celebrate
our 35th Wedding Anniversary together,
I pledge to continue my love for you.
It is strong, it is firm and it is sealed forever.
It does not change like the California weather.

If someone were to ask me, how long my love for you will sustain?
Papa will look up and smile, and tell them
*"Until God sends the latter rain."*

**I Love You, Mollie**

# Chapter 13

# TO GOD BE THE GLORY

Thanks to Tom's insatiable desire for researching our family roots, the family had been blessed to have a history of our ancestral heritage. Both Tom and Willemena always maintained a positive relationship with relatives both near and far away. They attended reunions, birthday parties, graduation ceremonies and family events whenever and wherever they occurred. We could always count on them to represent the Ware family by exchanging photos and obtaining updated addresses for the rest of us.

## THE ULTIMATE

The crowning achievement of Tom's contribution to the family was his handling of the sale of the homestead, 1201 "G" Street. Significantly, I was one month old when my mother carried me into, 1201 "G" Street. They had just purchased the house. The year was November 1930. I was sixty-one years old when Tom closed the deal on the sale of the property in 1991. At first, many of us had mixed emotions about the sale since we had experienced a lot of happy moments there. Both Maurice and I started our journey in life there. The sad feelings were short lived, when we realized the potential for financial gain from the sale. In 1930, our family had purchased 1201 for $6,000.00 dollars (which was a lot of money for us at that time). Over the years we struggled and worked to pay the monthly notes. Finally, we paid off the mortgage in 1949 (19 years later). We continued to grow up there and in the late 50's, most of the family had relocated out of D.C. Tom and our sister Doris remained. Tom was left with the responsible task of maintaining the property. In my passion, I had always wanted to buy 1201, and keep it in the Ware family for a lasting legacy. Unfortunately my financial status would not allow me to pursue my goal.

Shortly after we all left D.C., Tom started getting letters and calls from investors wanting to buy 1201. The family all voted to sell the property, since none of us had any intentions of relocating back to D.C. Tom was the lone dissenter. He kept saying we should not sell at the present time. The family asked me to fly back to D.C. and encourage Tom to sell. Both Mildred and I made Tom an offer if he would agree to sell the property as soon as possible, we would each give him 10% of our share of the sale. Tom said, "No deal." I remember saying to him, "Tom I need the money now! Mollie needs a new hat, and Teddy needs shoes, lets sell this property and all go on a cruise." Tom continued to say, "NO!" In fact, he boarded up the house and said we are going to wait!

## HE HAD INSIGHT

In retrospect, we can now say that Tom was truly a visionary. He sensed something unusual about all the real estate speculators trying to buy the property, and he was right on target.

Within the next six months, the city planners re-zoned the "G" Street area as the "Capital Hill Zone" which meant that the government workers could live in close proximity to the Capitol and would pay high prices for the real estate. Overnight the property values went up, and Tom said, "Now we can sell 1201."

It is ironic to note that our parents purchased 1201 for $6,000.00 and Tom sold it for six figures needless to say, we were all glad that Tom prevailed. It should be noted that the property had been vacant for a long time and was in need of major repairs. However, to his credit as a skillful negotiator, Tom sold the property "As is" thus saving us thousands of dollars. Tom had proven his real estate skills when he purchased, his Clinton ST property in 1951.

In October 1995, General Tom called on his troops to attend the Million Man March in Washington D.C. Some of us flew in from California, others drove in from Detroit, and some came from Chicago and Atlanta. Tom had said, "You should be at this march for the sake of your children. It's going to be a historical event." We all gathered at Tom's house and after he led us in prayer, we marched to the Capitol Mall, where the event started. It was awesome to witness the events at the march. Some brothers flew to the march; others rode horses and drove cars. Some came in busses and boats, and some even walked in from Maryland and Virginia. There was some initial dispute over the actual number of participants at the march. The park service flew over the area and took aerial photos of the group. They estimated nine hundred-eighty thousand, in attendance. This figure was later changed to over one million, when they re-considered the brothers sitting under the trees, and the statues, around the area.

Ancient African Tribal customs stipulated that our brothers used drumming to rally the natives and call them to meeting!! Such was the case on the night of October 18, 1995, when we all attended the Washington D.C. Convention Center for a mass rally. Rallies were held at churches throughout the city encouraging our brothers to respond to the march. At exactly 5:00 am, on the morning of October 19th, a group of young brothers assembled at the Capitol Mall, and started continuous drumming; this was a call for all African brothers to atone! At the same time that our brothers started drumming in D.C., our African brothers started drumming in Kenya and Nairobi, Africa. It was a coordinated effort to display unity for our brothers to march. It was truly a day of reconciliation for black men. I can still remember hearing the beating of the drums in a slow cadence.

I shall never forget the inspiration of being among one million of my brothers, and vowing, re-dedication to my family. I came back to California, ready to spread the word to our black brothers to do the right thing!! I created a scrap book of pictures and memorabilia from the march (a picture and an ad calling brothers to support the march is displayed in another chapter).

I want my grandchildren to see what we experienced during the march. At the close of the march, we were encouraged to be accountable to our families, refrain from using substance abuse, and stand up as real men. We were all asked to donate one dollar each, to defray the cost of the event. We were asked to hold the dollar up in the air and wave it, as a prayer of dedication was uttered. It was inspiring to witness the "Sea of Green" as one million brothers waved their donation and prayed. We then re-grouped at Tom's house for dinner (which he prepared); we critiqued the events of the day.

## MEMORIES

I would like to point out that this was Tom's second unified effort of support for a march in D.C. He had been instrumental in bringing the troops together for the 1963 Martin Luther King March in D.C. I was in the Air Force, stationed in N.C., and I could not get time off to attend. My niece, Yvonne Gastin marched for me!!

## TRUE POLITICAN

Tom had the political astuteness to guide us the right way. He was truly a general that knew how to lead his troops.

As the years went by and whenever there was a National Campaign for President of the USA, Tom would send us a mailer. In it he would outline the pros and cons of each candidate. He would close by saying, "Don't forget to vote." "I know you will make the right choice, I plan to vote for, _____!"

Yes, Tom was a remarkable individual. He was courageous, compassionate, witty and intellectual.

I am proud to have known him as my big brother, my friend and my leader. I have had to climb a lot of mountains and cross a lot of rivers in the past seventy-seven years of my life, and I thank Tom for helping me along the way. Although our sisters were older, he also helped them with car maintenance, moving and needed finances. Tom helped his brothers and his sisters.

## WE WERE LIKE THE CORSICAN BROTHERS

In many ways, Tom and I had similar experiences. For example we both left college to join the military. We both worked with equal opportunity programs. We both worked with the Department of Corrections. In fact, I was offered a position as, Director of Lorton Correctional Facility, but I declined when the Governor appointed me, Chairman of the Youthful Offender Parole Board, in California. Tom worked on the railroad, and I passed the test railroad mail clerk (but it was phased out). We both loved to travel, we both loved trains, we both loved our wives and we both loved the church.

As I reflect back on the Million Man March, we were admonished not to beat or batter our wives. I can testify assuredly that none of the Ware boys ever raised our hands to assault our sisters or our wives. We have a disdain for men who batter their wives. When we worked in the Criminal Justice System, we noted that prospective correctional officers who had a history of battering their wives or being cruel to animals, were not hired for fear that they might batter the inmates under their control. No one deserves to be battered. We were also taught that there are twelve signs of deviant behavior that identifies a potential batterer namely:

1. Jealousy
2. Blames others (including you for his/her faults)
3. Blames circumstances for their problems. ("If only I had a job, I wouldn't be so upset")
4. Unpredictable behavior
5. Belittles you verbally
6. Cannot control their anger
7. Always asks for a second chance
8. Claims that they will change and won't do it again
9. Their family resolves problems with violence
10. Will play off of your guilt. ("If you loved me, you'd . . .")
11. The behavior often worsens when alcohol and drugs are used
12. The person is closed minded; theirs is the only way

Neither, Tom, Maurice or I, ever exhibited any of these tendencies. Our strong church background helped us to overcome.

*"To God Be the Glory through Jesus Christ Forever"*
Romans 16:27

# Chapter 14

# WHEN THE SAINTS GO MARCHING IN

*"I will lift up mine eyes,*
*unto the hills from whence cometh my help"*
Psalms 121:1

I n our declining years, Tom and I often discussed what we should be doing to insure that our families would be stable and comfortable after our demise. We shared the locations of our safe deposit boxes, bank accounts, insurance polices and wills.

We talked about our final resting place and our funeral arrangements. Tom asked me to sing, "When the Saints Go Marching In" at his funeral. I was surprised to learn that two other people said he wanted them to sing the same song. None of us sang at the funeral because the planners had programmed a special New Orleans Celebration after the funeral in his honor. I was very pleased with the outstanding manner that his beloved god-daughter, and sister-in-law Sherby Miller and Eileen Boyd, as well as the parishioners of the historic Vermont Ave. Baptist Church conducted his funeral. It was a blessed event. A huge crowd of mourners attended his funeral. I counted thirty-two cars at his gravesite in Arlington Cemetery. The re-past after the funeral included many of his jazz followers. The program was held at his favorite eatery, the Takoma Station Restaurant. All those who attended were given handkerchiefs "In Memory of Tom 1929/2007."

## NUMBER ONE

Tom was the first Ware boy to enter this world and the first to leave it. He was first in our hearts and we sincerely miss him. Both Maurice and I needed our big brother. He devoted time, effort and money to promote a better way of life for us. He cared and he shared for us 24/7. In one sense, I believe that Tom was first because God knew that Maurice and I would have health problems and that we would need a leaning post. For example, I remember (at an early age) when the "G" Street Gang went on a trip to the Local Creek, to fish and wade in the water. While I was in the creek, I felt a sharp pain on my foot. I had stepped on a broken coke bottle and cut it. Tom took off his undershirt, wrapped up my foot and placed me on his shoulders and carried me home (a distance of approximately three miles).

The day before he passed away, Tom called me (but I was not home). I got his message off my answering service and decided that I would call him the next day. Unfortunately, he passed away before I could make the call. I decided to keep his cheerful greeting on my telephone answering tape. Tom had planned to visit us this summer and we were all planning to take a cruise to Hawaii in October.

As my son Ted and I started making plans to attend the funeral, the doctor had advised me to return to California within seventy-two hours. Since we missed attending the wake, the funeral director arranged a private viewing for me and Ted. As we viewed his remains, Ted said, "Dad look at the smile on his face, and look how sharp Aunt Willemena has him dressed." I said, "Yes, he looks like he is only sleeping." Then I realized what he had told me, "I'm going out of this world happy." I said it is like the fulfillment of prophesy. Amen.

Ted was very close to Tom. Actually, Ted was named after Tom. Ted is Thomas B. Ware and Tom was Thomas E. Ware. We were pleased when Willemena gave Ted a cap that Tom had made especially for him. As I looked down at my brother, I reflected on the seventy-eight years that God left him here to minister to us. I thought about how He:

A. Bailed me out of jail
B. Pulled me out of a gambling joint
C. Encouraged me to lose weight, diet and exercise
D. Encouraged me to study and get good grades in school
E. Stopped me from drinking cheap wine
F. Stopped me from dealing from the bottom of the deck!
G. Taught me how to budget and save money
H. Taught me how to fight to protect myself
I. Taught me how to get good jobs and how to work hard and faithful
J. Taught me how to be honest and do the right thing

To me Tom was always rated number one, like Hertz. I always rated myself number two, like Avis. Together we were the pride of our "G" Street peers.

In later years, Tom was instrumental in setting up living arrangements for Maurice in an outstanding care home. Maurice was happy with his (live-in) caregivers and he had his own private bathroom.

We were pleased to note that our cousin Lois Armistead had agreed to take him to his favorite church (Bibleway).

This is important, since Tom had to take the previous care home to court for improper handling of clients. Tom fought and won the right to have Maurice re-located into better facilities. Tom would make unannounced visits to the home and he would check the quality of the meals served. He made sure they took him on field trips to school and gave him a vacation each year. "Thank you Tom."

## FAREWELL MY BROTHER

As the Lord took Tom home, I can envision his saying, "Come home son, you have been a valiant warrior, you have carried out your mission and you have been an outstanding watchman for your brothers. Now you can rest in peace." Maurice is resting in peace and as I think about it, I too am in good hands, standing with me is my wife Mollie (54 years), my son Ted, along with Jasmine, Angelia, Diane, Brooks, Neice, Jackie, Jaden, Jordan, Alex, Rhonda, Jeanne, Tatiana and Parrish. We Are Family!

In closing, I have tried to capture much of the many faceted and inspirational incidents that occurred in the life and times of my brother Tom. I thank God for helping me to remember the time, place and sequence of the events, some as far back as seventy-five years ago. I challenge the remaining members of the Ware/Plater/Ellison family tree. Keep this book for your children and your children's children. Add your family experiences to it and let it all be a legacy for those who will follow us!

Tom was a well loved individual. Both he and his wife Willemena had been a positive influence to others down through the years. Tom was buried in Arlington Cemetery with full military honors. He is united with his two sons, Dexter and Kevin, whom he often talked about. As the tapes were played and as the rifles fired, I thought about Tom's transition to glory and I prayed, Lord Jesus,

"Welcome my faithful brother into your kingdom." He was the bridge that carried us over. He was the tower of strength that sustained us. He taught us to love you, as you loved him."

As I wiped away the tears, I said, "So long my big brother, soon, and very soon, I will see you on the other side!" I bowed my head, turned and walked away. Amen.

# HE IS ONLY SLEEPING

Shattering the silence of the still of the night

A call from our son gripped our hearts with fright

He wanted our granddad to continue living with us
but God told him to "get on the bus"

Through his recovery had been long fought our cries
and prayers were not for naught

His heart is still but free from pain

His eyes are closed, but he will see us again

If we live holy and free from sin

We are on our way to heaven and we will surely win

Yes he is only sleeping, and waiting for us

Someday we will join him and leave this earth to the dust

I can still hear him saying "I'm going upstairs"

I'm going to be with Jesus, because I know he cares

Get back Satan 'Cause I'm on a roll

I'm part of God's army of the brave and the bold

I'm working on my building and my bags are packed

I know for assurance that my Lord is coming back

You may ask me why I always sing

My answer is I'm waiting for Jesus our coming King

Sleep on Granddad, rest in the mansion upstairs

We will continue living holy, and we hope to join you up there

# The Life Sustaining Kidney Machine

As I sit in this chair watching the machine pumping my fluids out
I reflect back on how it all started with my severe case of gout.

Oh, how I wish I could reverse the early days of my life
When I didn't chew my food properly and I hardly ever used a
fork and a knife.

I was always grabbing junk food while I was on the run
I was impulsive and impatient
and would not stop until the job was done.

Little did I realize that haste makes waste,
Nor was I cognizant that abusing my body was not in good taste.

I was never concerned about adequate sleep and rest
I focused all my attention on getting rich
and making money to invest.

My only exercise was to run from job to job
Sometimes I slowed down to eat French Fries
and corn on the cob.

My wife kept warning me to eat food
that was boiled and not fried
But I kept loads of candy in my car
along with all the junk food I could hide.

She always prepared nutritious meals at home
But she could not control my ordering pizza on the phone.

I drank cokes and root beer morning, noon and night

But, I never acquired a taste for orange juice, milk and sprite.

My doctor kept telling me that my kidneys were failing
and the "get well ball"
Was in my court
Reality set in when I passed out in the Aruba airport.

I woke up in the hospital assigned to urgent care
My blood count was dangerously low and my vision was reduced
to a glassy stare.

Yes, this kidney machine is a sustainer of life
Actually it is just like having a second wife.

It tells you when your blood pressure is high or low
It warns you if there is an interference with your blood flow.

You have to use a warm blanket to stave off the chill
It takes three to five hours for your fluids to empty and refill.
I feel great when the treatment is over
and I rush to get something to eat
Only now I watch my diet closely limiting phosphorus and
potassium and eating more protein and meat.

The clinic provides me with a social worker, dietitian,
patient care technician, doctor and nurse
They all work in unity to insure
that the patient's quality of health come first.

They check your vital signs and monitor your heart
They inquire about your physical condition
and log it on your chart.

They check your skin and your access looking for danger spots
And, oh, yes they make sure that you get your share of flu,
T.B. and Hepatitis shots.

They provide you with a portable TV you can read,
listen to music or just sleep
You cannot use a cell phone, drink or eat
you will negate your purpose if you decided to cheat.

My wife offered to donate one of her kidneys to me
I thanked her as I rejected it, since my ordeal is temporary.

I am praying for a divine healing
as I sit here meditation on being made whole
This chair gives me ample time to pray
and wait for a miracle to unfold.

Meanwhile, I have adjusted to this machine
while waiting for my recovery
I am striving to make my health the best that it can be.

I firmly believe that I will be restored and set free
So I am thinking positive and taking sixteen day cruises
with dialysis at sea

# To my younger brother
# Charles Maurice Ware

There were (3) Ware boys, in our family. Tom was the oldest, I was in the middle and Maurice was the youngest. In his own quiet way, Maurice lived a holy and spiritual life. He was blessed to live under the watchful eye of a strong mother in Zion, "Mother Cora Ware." I shall always remember the words of Rev. Rufas Hayes Detroit Michigan, who said at her home going service, "If Mother Ware didn't make it to Heaven, the rest of us don't stand a chance of getting there."

Maurice demonstrated his love for Mother Ware, his brother and sisters, his Bibleway Family, and the Bibleway Church, on a daily basis. Of the (3) boys Tom was the strongest, the smartest, and the healthiest.

When Maurice was born, he had a serious health problem; however he was blessed with a strong sense of Mother wit and an extraordinary memory. An example of his Mother wit was his ability to think and challenge anything that left him in doubt.

When Tom got his first railroad job as a Traffic Cop, he proudly wore his uniform and badge. He playfully taunted Maurice, by saying "I am a Cop and I can arrest you." In his disbelief, Maurice followed Tom to work, hid behind some parked cars, and watched Tom direct the traffic. That evening he told Tom, "you're no Cop; I went to the Train Station, and I saw you blowing your whistle at the cars, and waving your hands, you're not no Cop!!" Maurice knew how to check things out.

At an early age Maurice was baptized in Jesus name, and saved. He always carried his bible to church, and he could turn to any one of the (66) books in the bible, that the Preacher was using as a text. One could sense that God was opening up his understanding of the scriptures while the message was preached.

An example of his keen memory was demonstrated when we were little guys. Our father gave us a box of candy, and Tom took a large share of it, I followed by taking a large share of it. This left Maurice with only a small amount of candy. About (6) months later, he walked up to us and hit us with a wooden board, we wanted to fight him, but we were taught not to hit Maurice. So we had to look at each other while he said, "That's for taking all my candy, you thought I forgot about it didn't you, I don't forget nothing?"

Maurice was blessed to have Mother Ware praying for him everyday. I can remember seeing her sitting by the living room window, watching and praying for his safe return home. While waiting, her favorite topics for discussion included The Bible, her noon day prayer service, Bishop Williams, Elder James Silver (now Bishop), her children, and Bibleway Church. I'm sure Maurice felt her prayers, because one night while he was sitting on the railing at the top of the steps, at Bibleway, he fell backward to the ground, (A distance of (21 Ft). He was blessed not to suffer any bruises, bumps, or broken bones, and he got up smiling, and saying "Thank you Jesus." Another example of his Mother wit occurred when I gave Mollie a new 1952 Chevy before going over seas in the Air Force. The car had Colorado plates. Maurice took the plates off and gave them to Mollie saying "This is Washington D.C., I have been watching my brother's car, and you need to change the license plates."

In closing, the Lord has called Maurice home, where he joins Mother Ware, Dad Ware, Bee, Grace, Doris, Helen and Tom, as they are walking around Heaven every day.

As the last surviving member of the first generation Ware's, you will find me saying "I will lift up my eyes unto the hills from whence cometh my help." Although, I have suffered through many operations, and I am on, Dialysis (3) days a week, I woke up last week saying "Though he slay me yet will I trust him."

"So long little brother, remember me as you crossover the River of Jordan, I look forward to being with you and the family, in Heaven someday."

"To God, Be the Glory"
Min. James Ware Jr.

# BIBLIOGRAPHY

(1) "If You Keep Laying Down with Dogs, You Will Get UP with Fleas"
American Actress Jean Harlow, 1944

(2) "40 Inspirational Saying for Fathers"
Unkown 1980

(3) Selected Poems, James Ware
"I'm Going Home on the Morning Train"
Author House, 2006

(4) Revels, Hiram Rhodes 1827-1901
Biographical Information of the U.S.
Congress, 1774-Present (page 1 of 1)

(5) Pinckney, Pinchback Officer and Politician
1837-1921
The African American Registry, 1990
Page (1 of 1)

(6) California's Dark Mother, The Mandate of Califia The Arthur
Wright, 2000
page 1-5

(7) Ebony Magazine- The New Black Father, July-2007

(8) Fatherhood, Bill Cosby A Dolphin Book
Doubleday and Co, 1986

(9) This is My Story Bishop S. Williams
Willoughby Publishers INC. 1981

# ABOUT THE AUTHOR

James J. Ware Jr. was born in Washington D.C. He has been married for (54) years, and has (5) children. He holds a Master Degree in Education, and a Bachelor of Science Degree in History. He is a (22) year retired Air Force Veteran. He has been writing poetry for (47) years and is listed in the National Library of Poets. After completing his military service he pursued the following occupations; Minister, Teacher, Legislative Consultant, Parole Board Chairman, Department of Corrections Ombudsman, and Charmain of his church Board of Directors.

He is the recipient of numerous awards in the fields of Military, Education, and Corrections.

James spends his spare time working with his grandchildren, writing poetry, playing computer Scrabble, researching Bible stories and listening to Classical and Gospel music.

# LIST OF COMPLETED PUBLICATIONS

"A History of the Air Force Reserve Officer Training Program at A&T College", N.C., 1963.

"Whatever Happened to Youth Authority Ward 1", A History of the First Youth Incarcerated in the California Youth Authority. 1979

"A History of the California Legislative Journey to Israel", 1975

"I'm Going Home on the Morning Train", A Book of Poetry 2006.

"A Story of the Disproportionate Number of Actions for Discipline with Minority Employees in the California Department of Corrections,"1999

www.ingramcontent.com/pod-product-compliance
Lightning Source LLC
Chambersburg PA
CBHW020236290526
45784CB00003B/1001